# *ETHICS AND SOCIAL RESPONSIBILITY IN BUSINESS*

*Harold A. Gram*

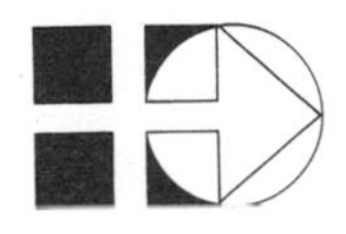

Concordia
Publishing
House
Saint Louis
London

Concordia Publishing House, St. Louis, Missouri
Concordia Publishing House Ltd., London, E. C. 1

Library of Congress Catalog Card No. 69-17598
MANUFACTURED IN THE UNITED STATES OF AMERICA

# *CONTENTS*

# *Preface*

Business ethics concerns us all, since we participate in the business system and are affected by the behavior of businessmen. The ethical behavior of businessmen affects our lives and the nation.

The modern businessman faces complex ethical decisions. He conducts his activities most often as a professional manager in a large organization, in an environment managed by the government, and in conflict with various pressure and power groups including unions, political parties, civil-rights organizations, and other business firms. The business firm is not only a producer of goods and services; it is a social system, a producer of social satisfactions for people connected with it, and tries to get things done through and with people. The government regards the firm as a social resource to be used for social goals and a good community.

The character of business ethics is more than the application of the Golden Rule. Ethical questions involve the conduct of business, social involvement, and the demands made on business by the government and social organizations. How far should the firm go in supporting the civil-rights movement? Should the firm use its profits to improve our cities? What does the firm owe the stockholders, the managers, the employees, the union, the suppliers, the community, and the customers?

This book approaches business ethics as it relates to the social responsibility of business. Business ethics that concerns itself only with the management of physical property and the application of honesty and integrity and is built on a capitalist concept of the economic system is inadequate for the type of social and ethical issues confronting the modern business manager.

It is the view of this author that ethical questions arise in business because the businessman is part of society. Ethical questions include the application of the standards of morality of the Ten Commandments but also the use of the power of the firm and the activities of the businessman in our social, legal, economic, and political systems. The behavior of the manager as he conducts his job, maintains the organization, seeks and accomplishes the goals of the organization, and gets results in its environment are important ethical concerns.

The Christian businessman, as he seeks justice and the preservation of the community, has to make many ethical decisions. He fulfills his Christian calling in a state of tension. Complex ethical questions and decisions arise as he views this world as the creation of God, people as God's creatures, and tries to serve.

My debt to many people prevents my listing them all. I do, however, want to express my appreciation to my wife and family for giving me the time to work, to my students at Valparaiso University for helping me formulate many of the ideas included here, and to my secretary, Mrs. Cheri Hill, who did the typing. I also want to acknowledge my gratitude to the American Management Association for giving permission to quote from Research Study No. 32, *Management Creeds and Philosophies*, © 1958.

# 1
# *Problems in Business Ethics*

The economic aspects of life are important to everyone. Each of us participates in the economic sphere as consumer of products, as wage earner, or as producer of goods and services. Through the business system we earn our income, receive the private goods and services that contribute to our welfare and well-being, and select the products we prefer. As participants in the economic process we are affected by the decisions and conduct of businessmen, the prime actors in the system. Questions of concern about their decisions involve us in business ethics.

We like to believe that our business system is producing all the goods and services of which it is capable and that the distribution of income and the utilization of resources are just, effective, fair, and efficient. We want to consume all we can and like to think we are getting as much of the total output as we can for our expenditure of effort and money. These beliefs and assumptions involve a concern with business ethics.

Businessmen occupy the central role in the economic system, which answers these economic questions: What is produced? How is it produced? Who produces it? Who gets what? How much is set aside in the form of capital for future production? The influence and control exerted by businessmen in the business system are concerns of business ethics.

*Popular Misconceptions of Business Ethics*

What may seem to be unethical business practices may often only seem so as a result of misconceptions and misinformation. Suspicions about business activities often reflect the rather low opinion of businessmen in general. The person familiar with literature may not dissociate the high prices charged by the small corner groceryman from the pound of flesh demanded by Shylock. When prices are "too high," we blame the businessman. But prices are often high because we are paying for the convenience of shopping at 12 midnight, because there is a shortage of supply, or because the prices are supported or set by government.

The banker is often compared with Scrooge of *A Christmas Carol* because he demands interest for a loan of money. We tend to ignore that the interest is payment for his services of providing loans and of keeping the accounts of his customers. His attitudes of prudence and care result from the confidence others have placed in him.

If we are stockholders and the stock market falls, we may have visions of greedy Wall Street bankers and brokers manipulating the market. Cries of "unethical," "immoral," or "robbing widows' savings" are often raised in these circumstances. The broker is not at fault if thousands of investors decide to sell because of rumors, a threat of war, or an announced policy of the government.

We tend to blame the wrong people for the wrong reasons. We may feel cheated by high prices, frustrated by the prying questions of the banker, and disappointed that our stock did not rise. But are these unethical practices? The charge of unethical practices is not an appropriate response to uncertainty. When the market responds to claims of war, gold losses, actions in other countries, or uncertainty concerning economic conditions at home, it is responding to uncertainty and risk. Not every high price the consumer pays or every loss an investor is unhappy about is directly attributable to bad business ethics.

We cannot blame the businessman for bad ethics when the operation of the economic process gives us depressions, booms, and prosperity. Nor can we decry as bad ethics high prices we must pay as a result of a shortage of goods and services.

Business ethics has to do with the way the businessman *conducts himself* as part of the economic system.

### *Personal Ethics and Business Ethics*

A distinction must be made between personal ethics and business ethics. The business community contains its share of immoral people, charlatans, impostors, "ten percenters," money grabbers, and drunkards. Such people are in every occupation of life, including the medical profession, the teaching profession, and the clergy.

Business ethics, however, is concerned with more than the personal weaknesses in the nature of man. There are as many moral, upright men in business as in any occupation. A distinguishing characteristic of the business system is that many kinds of transactions are conducted by word of mouth and in an environment of mutual confidence. It requires a high standard of personal ethics to exchange millions of dollars each day simply on the faith of another's word, nod, or telephone call, as is done in the stock and commodities markets.

The human problems of immorality and greed apply to the customer as well as the businessman. In the exchange of a used car, for example, the customer does not consider it wrong to unload a "lemon" on the used-car dealer, but he thinks it is wrong for the dealer to sell the same car to another person. The action of the dealer is more apt to be called a problem of business ethics than is the action of the customer.

James W. Culliton of Ohio State University can find general agreement for his proposition that there is "no evidence of basic conflict between business and ethics."[1] The business world does not demand a lower standard of personal morality than does any other position. The bad ethics of businessmen cannot be attributed solely to their being involved in business and dealing with money. Business is not the cause of immorality and false ideology, as Karl Marx believed on the basis of his theory of economic determinism. People's ethics are not determined by the way they earn their living.

Business ethics is concerned with the way the businessman, as a businessman, conducts his business. Business ethics is properly the ethics of doing business.

### *The Businessman and Business Practices*

The proper ethical concerns of business are the practices, procedures, and methods by which the businessman buys his resources, produces and sells his product, and earns a profit.

The Code of Ethics of Atlas Steels Limited of Welland, Ontario, illustrates this dimension of business ethics. "The Basic Policy of Atlas Steels Limited—To achieve as high a return upon investment as is possible, compatible with firm Christian principles, scrupulous honesty, and complete fairness to *all* people whom we contact—especially shareholders, employees, customers, and suppliers."[2]

Martin Luther observed the practices of businessmen and wrote in *On Trading and Usury* (1524): "For these three errors,—that everyone may sell what is his own as dear as he will, borrowing, and becoming surety, —these, I say, are the three sources from which the stream of abomination, injustice, treachery and guile flows far and wide: to try to stem the flood and not stop up the springs, is trouble and labor lost." [3]

Luther was concerned with prices, interest, and trading in the market. In addition to the bad practices listed above, he included cornering the supply, raising the price of goods sold on credit, raising prices because of scarcity, underselling, and dealing in futures. On another occasion (*Treatise on Usury*, 1520) Luther denounced the taking of interest. Although Luther thought that buying and selling were necessary, he felt that many business dealings were filled with greed, avarice, and wickedness.

Fair prices and fair wages have been concerns from the Middle Ages to the present. Attempts have been made to define a "fair price" by measuring the quantity of labor involved in the production of a product. Differences in the *quality* of labor have frustrated this approach. The current theory used to explain prices arises from marginal analysis, which holds that prices are determined by the operation of demand and supply. In a free market where demand and supply operate, the prices of products and wages are "fair."

The 1961 Electrical Conspiracy Case raised questions concerning the business practices of price collusion and evasion of the antitrust laws. The questions of what are "just" or "fair" prices have given way to a concern for the practices and procedures by which the price is set.

The early reformers saw the business ethical problem as the level of prices; the current business ethical concerns are with the process by which prices are established. The Electrical Conspiracy is considered an unethical practice not because the price of the product was too high but rather because the price was agreed on, the market was shared, and competition was absent.

Business ethics involves the business practices and procedures of the firm with its customers, its employees, and other business firms. What kinds of products may a firm sell? Does the market behavior of the businessman include an ethical responsibility for his customers' choices?

Should a businessman sell a product he knows is useless? Should a businessman mislead a customer? Should a businessman sell a product to a customer if he knows the customer cannot afford it? Whose responsibility is it to advise the customer if he elects to buy a product from another supplier rather than you, and you know the customer is getting a bad deal? What should be the nature of transactions between the businessman and his customers?

Business ethics includes the relationships of the firm with its employees. In a world of automation and advanced technology, should a businessman reduce his work force and discharge elderly people because the work can be done more efficiently by machine? Does an employer have the right to fire an employee without a fair hearing and without giving him a chance to defend himself? Should a farmer grow his crops with cheap labor performed by people who have entered the country illegally? What level of wages and what benefits does an employer owe his employees? How much work should one demand from an employee? How should one treat his employees when giving directions? Business ethics is concerned with what is just, fair, and equitable in practices and in wages affecting employees.

The relationships of employers to one another is another part of business ethics. How one treats his competitors and works in relationship with them or against them is an ethical concern.

Business ethical practices are involved as the small competitor tries to compete with a large competitor. Does the large competitor have the right to force a small producer out of business by using his ability to sell at a cheaper price? What are the limits of fairness and equity when the law of competition degenerates into the law of the survival of the fittest? How does a small competitor compete against house brands (brands produced by a major producer but sold under the name of a store) when he must sell exactly the same product as a name brand at a higher price? Does a businessman have the right to tell his customers about the unethical practices of fellow businessmen? Do competitors in a smaller community have the right to engage in collusion and special agreements?

Current questions of business practices and business behavior in the marketplace, the firm, and with one another are properly the area of business ethics.

*Business Ethics as Social Responsibility*

More recently the problem of business ethics has been focused on socially responsible behavior and the social responsibilities of businessmen. The business firm is both an economic and a social unit. It does exercise power in the community in which it operates. The businessman may treat his employees ever so well, but does he have any responsibility for providing employment in the area in which he operates?

It is one ethical problem to treat an employee in a certain way, but does one have the responsibility of providing jobs for those who are currently unemployed? The problem becomes even more complicated if the unemployed are unskilled, undisciplined, and require a long period of training.

The corporation does have power, but does it have any ethical responsibility to use its power to further the cause of civil rights or the public welfare? The large corporation may be honest and fair with its employees, but does it have responsibility for the current issues of public policies, such as clean air, safe and clean water, and making the environment decent and healthy?

This issue is often discussed under the general heading of the social responsibilities of businessmen. Because business conducts its activities in relationship with customers, suppliers, unions, other corporations, the public, the community, and the underdeveloped countries of the world and affects them, it is believed by many that business has responsibilities to these various groups. The character of business ethical responsibilities is felt to be broader than honesty or good business practices. It includes social action or social involvement, programs for community development, and support of the values and goals sought by people as individuals or groups. Questions surrounding the social responsibility of business have come from several major concerns.

In meeting the goals of full employment, high production, purchasing power, and economic growth, government sees the firm as a social asset to be used for the accomplishment of desirable social ends. What, then, are the ethical responsibilities of business as good corporate citizens in the country and in the community? What kind of activity should the firm undertake to meet and to assist in the accomplishment of goals set by government and considered desirable for the welfare of society?

The great social power and size of business has raised the question of the ethical use of that power. As long as the firm is considered only an economic unit, one can discuss its ethical roles in relationship to the economic system. However, as soon as the firm is examined as a behavioral unit or social system, different kinds of ethical questions arise. Elbing and Elbing raised the issue: "It is precisely from the nature of business as a social system that the value issue of business must be formulated."[4]

The large corporation is the representative institution of modern business. In 1959, 66 percent of all corporate wealth was owned by the 500 largest corporations. In 1954 only 3.8 percent of all manufacturing establishments employed 250 people or more, yet they accounted for 59 percent of all employees and produced 64 percent of all value added in manufacturing. These large concentrations of economic power can be controlled only by that which is larger than they are.

The firm does exercise social power. The question is, How and to what purpose shall its social and economic power be used in the interests of the welfare of mankind?

Many of the ethical questions confronting businessmen relate to the role of the large corporation in society. What responsibility does the firm have to the slums at its doorstep? What responsibilities does it have to the poorer nations of the world? How shall it dispose of its profits? Should it support education, charitable foundations, or other worthwhile social projects? What are the dimensions of its responsibilities for the welfare of society in producing good products and in the discretionary uses of its income?

*The Manager and Ethics*

Business ethics includes the ethics of management behavior. The modern business firm is directed by managers who make decisions. How business managers conduct their functions involves ethical considerations.

Chester Barnard has pointed out that a significant dimension of modern business is its representative character. The executive working in a business is often not an owner of the business. He is part of an organization; yet he exercises the power of ownership. The manager operates with rules and procedures he did not establish. He tries to accomplish goals he did not choose and works with people he has not selected. Like the worker, the executive is separated from the final product of the firm and made a part of an organization.

The business executive who lives in suburbia is part of this organizational society. Business ethics for him concerns his behavior in an organization in which he performs a job assigned to him. He does not set the general goals of the company. He may never see a customer if he manages the accounting division or the computer center. His relationships with other employees and the employer are often established by union agreement. He produces no product that is sold to the ultimate consumer but performs a service that maintains the organization.

The problems of business ethics that concern the business executive directly are often those related to his life in a large organization, as William H. Whyte Jr. shows in *The Organization Man.* How does he remain an individual in business and at the same time carry out the wishes of the organization for the accomplishment of its goals? What kind of ethical standards are applicable —a social ethic or an individual ethic?

The organization, Whyte believes, demands a particular kind of social ethic which seems to conflict with his personal ethic. The social ethic has three major propositions: "a belief in the group as the source of creativity; a belief in 'belongingness' as the ultimate need of the individual; and a belief in the application of science to achieve the belongingness." [5]

Amitai Etzioni observes that the organizational dilemma is "between organization needs and personal needs; between rationality and nonrationality; between discipline and autonomy; between formal and informal relations; between management and workers; or more generally, between ranks and divisions." [6]

The ethical dilemma of the manager in the business environment arises from his being a manager—one who makes decisions. Within an organization his concerns are for the organization, and many of his goals are those of the organization. He occupies a peculiar place within the organizational structure and performs a particular function.

Peter Drucker pointed to the product of our organizational revolution in his statement that not the individual but the organization is productive.

The manager has considerable discretion in making decisions involving value. His problem is one of professional behavior within an organizational structure. The concern for managers in business is "ethics as responsible professional behavior."

The ethical questions confronting the modern manager arise because he is part of a system in which he operates in groups, performs a function, and can serve the ultimate purposes of the organization only through mutual interaction and cooperation.

Theodore V. Houser stated the ethical problem in *Big Business and Human Values:* "What actually happens to the individual is ultimately determined not by the free play of a market, but by the administrative process of an organization." [7]

IBM

# 2

# *The Changing World of Business*

The ethical problems confronting the Christian in business have changed as the structure, organization, and operation of business have changed. Modern business has replaced the individual inventor with the research and development department and the entrepreneur with the organization. The business structure does not correspond to the capitalistic model of society on which we have based many of our ethical judgments and directions in the past. The newer ethical problems grow out of the recognition that modern business is characterized by organizational life, management behavior, and discretionary decision-making. The nature of our ethical problems has changed because modern business is no longer conducted only under the rules of capitalism but as part of a managed and directed economy. Elements of the capitalist economy remain as long as people can make choices, competition prevails between firms and individuals, profit-making is prevalent, and a large measure of freedom prevails in marketing and employment. This change from a completely capitalist economy to a managed, mixed free-enterprise economy has brought with it different kinds of ethical questions.

### *Ethics in a Capitalist Society*

In the capitalist structure of society, goods and services are under private ownership and control. The level of output, the distribution of goods and services, and the quantity of goods and services consumed collectively or individually are determined by decisions made by individuals in the private sector of the economy. Individuals have choices of occupations, goods and services, or opportunities. This structure, called the free enterprise system, is peculiarly American and can be traced to the times of the Reformation. As one of its features it has, as John A. Hobsen says, the capitalist spirit, or the capacity to apply accumulated wealth to profit-making.

This system is built on two major philosophical foundations—the right of private property and the right of contract. Business is considered a private matter, whether organized as an individual proprietorship or as a corporation. In the corporation the shareholders provide capital for the organization of the firm; the managers operate the firm; and the customers through the operation of a free market have a choice of the products they prefer.

The manager in the corporation is in a direct relationship between shareholders and customers. The corporation exists and comes into being as people band together and freely form an organization to profit from specialization and the division of labor. Whatever the particular role a person occupies within the firm, his relationships are always very clear: shareholders⟶ managers⟶customers.

The right of private property and the right of contract provide a basis for the corporation and determine the relationships with employees and with other business firms. Employees are assumed to join the firm as a result of their free will and to have the freedom to leave. Freedom of contract is expressed not only by the people who form the corporation but by the people who are free to remain associated with the firm or to leave it. The early use of child labor in the factories of Britain was defended on the basis of the right of people freely to work where they wanted: the child had made a contract with the employer, and it was the latter's responsibility to direct his effort.

The capitalist concept of business gives a special dimension to the problem of business ethics. The managers, operating in the interests of the stockholders, are to act as good stewards of the property entrusted to them by the stockholders and to secure the maximum return. Like the man in the parable of the talents, they are to see that the firm is run efficiently. To accomplish these purposes, they are to combine resources in their most profitable combinations and care for the customers. A measure of their success is found in the profit earned by the firm.

The capitalist concern with efficiency is comprehended within the economic theory of profit maximization. A manager is directed to combine the inputs of the firm in their most profitable combination. Economic theory supports efficiency by asserting that resources should be combined until marginal cost equals marginal revenue. The paramount importance of efficiency in the capitalist and free enterprise ideology made it possible to build sophisticated rational economic structures that seem to provide answers to every problem. Efficiency is carried over into management theory by scientific management.

The ethical standards for the behavior of businessmen in such a capitalistic society are no different from those required of any other person. Adherence to the Golden Rule, of which J. C. Penney became a well-known example, determines relationships with customers. The business firm is comparable to the individual in the marketplace. As the individual seeks to get all he can for his money, so the businessman should act in the same way.

The growth of a capitalist society and its development are rooted in the initiative, ambition, and desires of people. It seeks to harness human selfishness for the common good. There is no doubt that capitalism as an economic system has provided for a rapid growth in the quantity of products available, for change, and for much of the strength of American economic society.

There is a close relationship between the Protestant ethic and the spirit of capitalism, as Max Weber showed in his study of the problem. The Protestant ethic is used to describe the favorable attitudes toward hard work, frugality, independence, the prudent use of wealth, personal acquisition, private property, and profit attitudes traceable to the Protestant Reformation. It is an ethic for behavior in the secular world that arises from the Protestant doctrine of individual responsibility, direct relationship to God, and a concern for the welfare of this world.

The Protestant ethic seems to coincide with the needs of capitalism for freedom of initiative, a spirit of personal acquisition, and a belief in private property. As it expresses itself in a concern for hard work, frugality, service and obedience to God, and a concern for the stewardship of possessions, it supports a capitalistic society. Capitalism is built on business as a private matter. This companionship of mutual interest has led many people to believe that capitalism and Christianity are directly related to one another. They see in capitalism a respect for private property, initiative, and individual responsibility that accords with the meaning of the Ten Commandments and the opportunity for stewardship. Capitalism has also flourished in a democratic society and in many respects is the economic side of democracy. The equating of capitalism, Christianity, and democracy by many people has led to the impression that God could be spelled Get and that self-interest is equivalent to Christian love.

The ethical questions confronting the businessman who holds the concepts of capitalism are related to his use of private property and the ethics of the adherence to contracts already formed or that could be formed. Questions of the businessman's relationships with his employees could be answered by insisting that if an employee felt he wasn't being paid enough, he could always leave. Was it not of divine concern that one tried to increase what God had given him? Was it not the employee's and employer's divine responsibility to work as hard as they could? The canons of decency and honesty directed the producing of a good product. The individual was free to choose or reject the product. Honesty was the best policy, as it was for every individual in his behavior with other people.

Anything, including government, that interfered with the exercise of the right of private property not only contributed to inefficiency but was unethical, according to this view. Some people have opposed income tax and Social Security on the grounds that they steal from the wealthy and give to the poor. To many people there is no distinction between the ethics of Christianity and of capitalist behavior.

Other ethical questions in a capitalistic view of business relate to business practices and business behavior. The Christian standards of individual behavior are held to be sufficient guides for directing one's relationships with customers, employees, and competitors. The advice of John Wesley that "we must exhort all Christians to gain all they can and save all they can" seems acceptable not only as a good ethical guide for religion but for one's behavior in the business world.

This view of business was held by such men as John D. Rockefeller and Stephen Girard, to mention but two. Girard at death left the bulk of his estate to the city of Philadelphia as a sign of his personal trust and stewardship. Rockefeller was not ashamed to relate that his success in the Standard Oil Company was due to the operation of the law of the survival of the fittest and that he overcame competition because he was the stronger. This, he explained, is not an evil tendency but a working out of the law of nature and the law of God. His success, he explained, was due to his own election by a fair and a just God.

Underlying the capitalist system of production and consumption is a philosophy of work. Between the individual and his ability to consume lies the moral imperative of work for all. The income a person receives arises from the work he performs, and his income makes it possible for him to consume goods and services. One can express this in a formula by writing C (consumption) depends on Y (income), which depends on W (work): $C=f(Y)=f(W)$. The effective operation of the capitalist system depends on motivating people to work, as the Protestant ethic does. The words of St. Paul were used to lend support to this system: "If any would not work, neither should he eat." (2 Thessalonians 3:10)

*Private Interests and Public Welfare in a Capitalist Society*

The public welfare is not a direct concern of business according to those who view business as part of a capitalistic structure. The effective operation of both competition and individual self-interest produces the public welfare. The government has responsibility for national defense, police, the support and establishment of laws, and the care of certain kinds of people. Questions of the national interest and welfare are to be handled by the government.

The individual in capitalism is considered to be the basis of society—from him comes the government, society, and business. In this view it is really not the fault of business if people prefer products that may hurt them. People determine what business produces, who should produce it, and in what quantities. As knowledgeable people are given a choice, have alternatives, and can select in a free market, the public welfare is furthered, and bad practices are driven out.

The economic system can exist and function only in complete freedom. Like a great machine that can keep running only with freedom and choice, the best society is one in which each person minds his own affairs, makes his own choices, and pursues his own interests.

In the market, bad practices are primarily the result of an absence of competition. The improvement of ethics requires only an improvement in the structure of the market by removing monopolies and hindrances to competition. The theory is that in a free market people would not be misled for long. Each businessman operates with the fear of failure, since his customers can always go to a competitor. Consequently, in the interest of his own survival, the businessman treats customers fairly, honestly, and justly. The free market determines who produces the product and what products. Questions related to the social welfare are answered by a confidence and faith that a product manufactured by a firm that earns a profit is socially desirable. The market can answer the social questions for employees, employers, other competitors, consumers, and the country concerning the quantity of product, the quality of product, and whether more money should be allocated to schools or churches, to beer or religion, or to national defense or television sets.

In this competitive world it is not possible for the businessman to earn too high a rate of profit, according to this view. If he does earn too much profit, other competitors will take away some of his customers by producing an identical product.

In the long run all firms would earn only enough profit to keep themselves in business. Profits can be justified by business as rewards for hard work, thrift, industriousness, and the application of the grace of God.

Whether too much is being spent on consumer goods and not enough given to the churches is a question the businessman can answer by saying that he satisfies the wants of the people. If the public welfare is not being pursued, it is the fault of government. The public welfare always results from perfect or free competition. The cry of the free-enterprise economy is: "Always let the people decide."

Support for this kind of business system is provided by Milton Friedman and others. Concerned with the matter of capitalism and freedom, they believe that business ethics is the application of the Golden Rule or face-to-face civility and profit maximization. The National Association of Manufacturers states in *Moral and Ethical Standards in Labor and Management:*

> Individual freedom and the sanctity of the individual stem directly from God and we should guard these gifts as our most precious possessions. God has given men the privilege and responsibility

to pilot their own lives without undue controls and coercion. . . . Corporate management has a solemn obligation to the individual stockholders who have saved and risked their money. . . . Effective, free, and open competition is the basic regulating and directing force in our economy. It serves the public interest and provides products to consumers at the lowest possible prices.[1]

*The Economic Base of Capitalism*

The theoretical structure of this kind of system was provided by economists, first by Adam Smith and then by such men as Alfred Marshall. A market economy is best described by a diagram referred to as the "wheel of wealth."

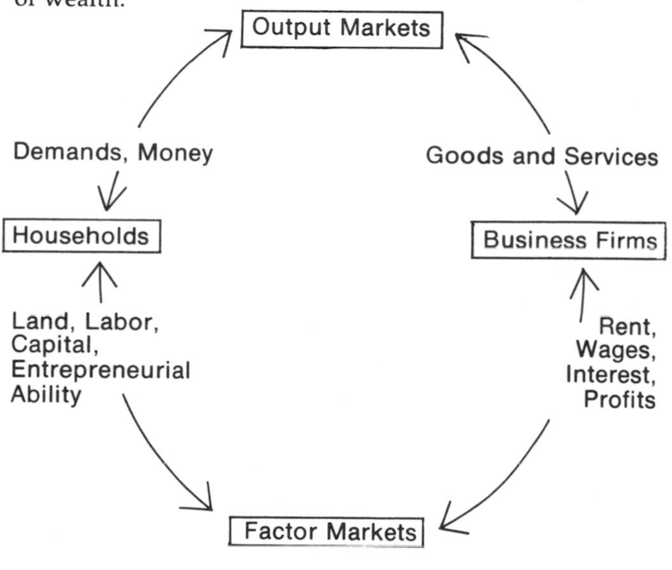


**Diagram 1**

The output markets include all goods and services produced and sold in the economy. Prices are set by the operation of demand and supply. The factor markets include land, labor, capital, and the market for all inputs used to produce the product. People express their preferences in markets and offer their services in markets.

So long as the markets are free, the existing prices of products can be explained by demand and supply. The price of labor or interest can be defended as resulting from market forces. Businessmen are able to say that the market, not they, sets prices. Wages can be defended by appealing to the low or high productivity of labor, the existence of competition, or the willingness or unwillingness of people to work.

This system explains the poverty of some and the high income of others in terms of market forces. Some people have skills not demanded by business. Some lazy and indifferent people could have higher incomes if they worked more. Others are wealthy because they work hard, have the appropriate skills, and know better how to manage their money.

The business manager acts ethically if he uses resources efficiently, satisfies people's demands, maximizes profit as a good steward of the capital of the stockholders, and obeys the ethics of competition.

Certain ethical problems arise from government activity. Government interference with the rights of private property and of contract, with competition, and with the operation of the free market will interfere with the ability of the businessman to act as a good steward and with the people's freedom of choice and use of their incomes.

For this economic system to operate efficiently, several conditions and assumptions must be satisfied:

—There must be a direct relationship between the ownership of the business firm and the stockholders.

—The markets must be free, that is, with no monopolies or large concentrations of economic power.

—The firm must restrict itself solely to its role in the economic sphere, that is, to the production and distribution of goods and services.

—Firms must produce the goods and services people desire and want, and the business firm must respond only to people's preferences.

—One must assume that people always know what they want and what is best for them and that they can express their desires and select from alternatives.

—One must assume that the public welfare always comes as a result of competition between people and cannot or should not be pursued directly. Competition is considered the best kind of relationship between one person and another and between one businessman and another.

—Businessmen are concerned only with economics, that is, the production and distribution of goods and services and with the stewardship of financial assets.

*Capitalism and Our Modern Business System*

Some insist that capitalism is the kind of system that ought to exist because of its foundation on efficiency, individuality, and privateness. But studies of modern business reveal that our economy is not a purely capitalistic society but a mixed economy. The economic model of capitalism does not adequately describe the complexity of our current business system. Our system includes not only significant elements of the capitalist structure, such as markets, profits, private property, and contracts, but it includes many more considerations.

Thus the economic model of pure competition, although useful for illustrating economic processes, cannot become the guide for moral and ethical decisions. Any attempt to deal with business ethics today must consider the mixed economy of our present society and cannot be based on concerns of a pure capitalism that no longer exists. Business ethics must be related to the structure of our modern business system.

American society over the past years has created a mixed economy composed of private and government production, private and government management, and an intermingling of social and economic matters. There is no absolute distinction between what is public and what is private.

There is a tenuous relationship between the manager and the owners of a large business firm.

Our markets are characterized by large concentrations of economic power in which oligopolies, monopolies, and government all participate in the production and distribution of goods and services. Oligopolies are large firms that have few competitors.

The business manager along with his firm is involved in welfare work, aid to education, and government assistance. The firm is more than merely an economic resource. It influences what and how much people buy and the society in which it operates.

Business firms produce and market products and in so doing lead people to upgrade their preferences and desires as well as accept new products.

The public welfare is a direct responsibility of the government, which pursues this by aid programs of various kinds, monetary and fiscal policy, and the management of the economy. Our modern business system does not accord with the economists' model of an efficient organization.

The following chart illustrates how our modern business system is different from pure capitalism:

**Decisions in Capitalism and Modern Business**

| *Economic Activity or Question* | *Pure Capitalism* | *Modern American Business* |
|---|---|---|
| What is produced? | Decided by people's preferences expressed in a market | *Decided by:* People's preferences in a market + Government + Managers in a business firm |
| How much is produced? | Decided by people's preferences in a market | *Decided by:* People's preferences in a market + Government monetary and fiscal policy + Managers |
| Who will produce goods and services? | Determined by people's choice of products | *Decided by:* People's choice of products + Government + Social and economic power of unions, government, and other firms |

| | | |
|---|---|---|
| Who will get available output? | Decided by those who have income from work | *Decided by:* Those who have income from work + Government monetary and fiscal policy + Progressive income tax + Welfare programs + Collective bargaining ability or power + Political process |
| Prices | Decided by a free market | *Decided by:* Markets + Government + Collective bargaining |
| Manager | Responsible only to stockholders and customers | Responsible for the maintenance of the organization and for society |
| Object of Business | Economic production of goods and services | Economic production of goods and services + Social resource for government goals + Maintenance of organization |

| | | |
|---|---|---|
| Structure of Business | Ideally small and competitive | Large concentrations in size and power, competition |

These changed characteristics form the basis for different kinds of ethical decisions.

*The Changed World of Modern Business*

Modern business is carried on in an environment dominated by the large firm, the corporate form of organization, the employment of the professional manager, and the active role of government. Modern business is characterized by the rise of the manager.

Economists and others have pointed to the existence of concentrations of firms within many industries and the billion-dollar firm. Companies like Sears Roebuck with sales in the billions dominate department-store retailing. In automobiles General Motors, Chrysler, and Ford are all billion-dollar companies. Although the number of small individual proprietorships is large, in food sales, retailing, and manufacturing the large firm is the representative organization of modern business. Fifty percent of all manufacturing is currently produced by the 150 largest corporations.

The corporate form of organization dominates American business. Large manufacturing organizations are modern necessities because of technology, which demands large quantities of capital, and because of the great needs for specialized skills in industry. Mergers and combinations have brought firms together in order to take advantage of economics in production.

Studies of American industry have shown that the large corporation has resulted in a separation of ownership and control. Those who control the firm are not the stockholders, who own the firm, but the professional managers who operate it. In 1967 American Telephone and Telegraph had 2,800,000 shareholders. General Motors shares of stock are spread out among 1,418,000 people. Standard Oil of Indiana has 173,000 shareholders. Stockholders meet to elect the board of directors, but effective control of the organization is undertaken by the officers and the staff of the corporation. The modern organization is autonomous, self-perpetuating, and self-organizing. Stockholders purchase the shares of the company for the return they get on their investment. If they are dissatisfied with the performance of the company, they can always, and often do, sell their shares.

The manager may be hired and fired without ever meeting any of the stockholders. He becomes a part of a self-directing organization that determines its own goals. The corporation exists as a fictional person in "contemplation of the law," which permits it to go its own way, employ, hire, and fire people, and make its own decisions.

The behavior of a large firm in the market cannot be compared to the action of an individual. The firm as an organization is not only different from an individual, but it also has more power, influence, and impact. Only competition from other large firms affects it. Competition is across an entire range of products. The large firm may suffer a loss for a long period of time, yet continue to exist.

The existence of large firms, the changed nature of competition, and the loss of a "free market" have prevented the marketplace from determining social values. John Kenneth Galbraith has criticized the American economic system for its inability to provide as many social goods (such as education, recreation, and roads) as private goods (like cars, refrigerators, and air conditioners). Our affluence has made us very rich in goods and services that are produced and selected privately, but poor in things that are produced and consumed collectively. Galbraith questions the ability of the consumer to determine social values within a market designed to express individual preferences and allocate private goods.

Public goods such as parks, roads, better education, and police protection do not compete in the market on the same terms as automobiles and stoves. To say that people prefer cars but no roads, or beer to education because they have not selected these is not true. The choice of social goods is made through the political process and not the economic system.

The large firm effectively makes a market for most of its products and does not fail each time it produces a product people do not want. The Ford Motor Company was able to absorb the failure of the Edsel in 1958 and still survive. The large corporation, with its large resources, diversified products, and varied markets, reduces the ability of any one group of consumers to control or determine its existence.

The large organization decides on a product and markets it. It does not respond simply to people's preferences and demands. In marketing, advertising is an essential ingredient to create consumer demand and acceptance. By market research the firm investigates people's preferences and then plans to meet them. It influences buying behavior by continually educating people to new products and their uses. Advertising is designed not so much to give information about a product as to create a desire to buy by appealing to people's motivations for prestige, status, selfishness, greed, or need.

The firm sees its total function as creating a consumer rather than simply responding to the demands of people. The "total-marketing concept" of modern business places the emphasis on organizing the firm for the purpose of selling its product.

The ability of the consumer to control the output of the large firm is limited. The consumer has limited alternatives, knowledge, and power. The power of the consumer is exercised in his choice of products available in the market but does not extend to initiating new or different products or deciding who will produce them. Where the capitalist system views the firm as responding to people's preferences, the modern business firm is actively trying to change and lead people's preferences. In the view of many people our business system is not controlled by consumer sovereignty.

The economic production of goods and services is also undertaken by monopolies, whether natural or contrived. The electric power company in most communities, though operated privately, is regulated by the government. In the interests of the common welfare, railroads are also regulated; it would be intolerable for railroad tracks to run all over the country and through various parts of our cities. Trucks and their routes are controlled and regulated.

Economic activity is not carried on with unbridled use of private property and the right of contract. Government regulations on zoning affect the use of property. Government regulates the operation of motor vehicles by licensing. Through the Securities and Exchange Commission it establishes controls on the sale of stock. These examples can be multiplied.

In the Unemployment Act of 1946 the government asserted that it will manage the economy to produce desired levels of output, employment, and prices. The Federal Reserve System controls the quantity of money and the availability of credit. It fixes interest rates to control inflation, investment, and mobility of capital. The government varies both the tax rate and government expenditures to accomplish desired output levels. The government uses its power and ability to affect economic activity by regulation, the progressive income tax, and executive decisions.

Economic activity and business are carried on in an economy managed by the government. This system allows opportunities for private choice and the exercise of competition, but choice and competition are not absolute and do not form the base of all economic activity.

*The Firm as a Social System*

Those who advocate the pure capitalistic system believe that the firm is only an economic unit and should perform only economic activities. In our present society the firm is both an economic unit and a social system. The firm not only produces goods and services but also social satisfactions, because it is an organization. Whatever its size, a modern business firm consists of people working and reacting with one another. They form a social system that embraces all human responses, desires, ambitions, and frustrations. The business firm as an organization provides satisfactions for creativity, social contacts, desire for new experiences, and for professional development. The firm does more than hire the services of people; it hires their time and their lives for a period of time. People cannot be separated from their labor.

The early view of the corporation as an extension of the right of private property saw the firm as an extension of stockholders' private property. Under this view it was logical therefore that management was entirely concerned to increase efficiency, expand output, direct the behavior of employees, and establish a rational organization.

In every organization today the manager is not managing quantities of labor; he is leading and motivating people. Management's increased efforts for efficiency can be frustrated by rumor, gossip, the social structure, and people's behavioral responses. People will produce if given the proper leadership. They have desires besides money. As human beings they want recognition, security, compatible colleagues, and a pleasant environment in which to work.

This behavioral view sees the firm as an organization with more than the single goal of economic output. It has many goals. The manager knows that because he is working with people he cannot be guided solely by profit maximization and efficiency. The firm does more than produce output; it produces social satisfactions for those people connected with it, and social welfare for the community.

The manager can accomplish the goals of the firm only through and with people whose reactions are conditioned by their goals, preferences, values, and the organizational setting. He manages not only financial assets but leads and motivates people, who are part of the total assets of the firm.

The social-system approach has changed the role of the manager. He is doing more than exercising a financial stewardship of the stockholders' money. The employees as well as others have an interest in how the firm is operated and managed. Many of their goals can be met only as the firm is maintained and operated. It is of interest to the employee how power is exercised as well as how it is selected. The manager knows that he can accomplish his purposes and the goals of the firm only as he is able to elicit the support, cooperation, and acceptance of his authority by the members of the firm.

The manager's role is motivating and leading people. Loyal, dedicated, and competent employees, as real assets of the firm, cannot and ought not be treated in the same way as machinery or financial assets.

Personnel departments were started to secure people for jobs but have assumed the social function of fitting the proper person into the proper job. Firms are concerned not only with hiring people but also with their placement within the business structure. The personnel department's function is to place people in the areas, jobs, and locations where they can produce to the best of their ability and find personal satisfaction.

The firm can be successful in the economic sphere only as it moves its real resources—its people and financial assets—toward desirable goals. The function of management is not only to represent the stockholders' interests but to provide satisfactions and meet the goals of people as they participate in the firm.

*Government and the Social Welfare*

The social interest has become accepted as a direct goal of government. The Employment Act of 1946 established the policy that government is to be concerned with a high level of production, output, and purchasing power. This goal involved the utilization of monetary and fiscal policy, that is, variations in the quantity of money and variations in government expenditure to secure the level of national growth and output that was desired.

In accomplishing these goals the government has

employed all means at its disposal. Contrary to the capitalist view that people should be able to consume only as a result of work, government has made direct gifts and grants to the sick and infirm and to those who are able to work but cannot find jobs.

The social interest has meant not only a concern for the unfortunates of society but for the unemployed, the underprivileged, and those who are unable to participate in American prosperity through consumption. As the government pursues the public interest, it affects the distribution of income and allocation of output.

The management of the economy by government rejects the idea that the private marketplace is to make all decisions regarding total output of the economy, its distribution, and its utilization. The government encourages the growth of some sectors of the economy and engages directly in other activities. Examples are housing, public transportation, control of highways, and regulation of air pollution and water pollution.

In accomplishing its goal of the public welfare, the government has restricted the absolute rights of private property and private contract. It has looked to the corporations as partners in accomplishing desirable social goals and as a social resource to be used. The managerial and technical abilities possessed by the business firm and the business firm itself are seen by the government as valuable social resources—as valuable as such natural resources as land, water, and minerals—for the meeting of social goals, such as reduced unemployment, slum clearance, and clean air. Government advises corporation management on setting of prices, especially for automobiles, steel, and aluminum. Contracts for corporation mergers, for example, are restricted by the Anti-Trust Division of the Justice Department.

*The Rise of the Manager*

Modern organizations have brought with them the rise of the managerial class. Men in the managerial group do not own the firm but are employed by the organization, receive salaries related to their position within the company, and control the operation of the firm. John K. Galbraith refers to these as the "techno-structure of American industry." Managers sell their services and earn their salaries not by producing a product but by their skill in combining the services of others to accomplish organizational goals.

The manager in business does not operate from a base of private property. His allegiance and devotion is to the organization, not to the stockholders. In his role he fulfills many of his own personal goals and at the same time determines or assists in determining the course and goals of the organization.

The income of the manager is related not to the quantity of work he produces but to his ability to progress within the organization and, through the practice of the skills of cooperation, social relations, and human reactions, to meet the goals of the organization. His progress in and worth to the company are not a result of his efficient utilization of property but of his utilization of human and social skills.

The manager, however, is not a professional in the strict sense of the term. His background may be in science, engineering, music, or some other field. He is a manager because he is able to get things done through and with people.

The manager affects the lives of people and their incomes through promotions, demotions, or job assignments. The goals of the firm are set by the management as are also the means to accomplish them. The focus of modern management is decision-making. The manager is limited in his discretionary behavior by some constraints, such as other firms, people's preferences and goals, and technological limitations. He does have control over many areas, such as the setting of prices, the structure of the organization, the product produced, how the profit is distributed, and for which purposes the resources of the organization will be used.

The ethics of modern management involve the relationships with people in organizations, decision-making, and relationships with society.

*Business and Its Commitments*

The rise of the large business organization, the decline of the role of the private market, the increasing concern of government for the social welfare, and the rise of the manager have changed the character of business. These changes raise new and different ethical questions and add an expanded dimension to business ethics. Business conducts its activities within a system that includes other power groups, such as unions, professional associations, and other large organizations that oppose its exercise of power. Decisions concerning wages and salaries are conducted in a collective-bargaining process; decisions on prices are supervised by government, and its power in these and other areas is regulated by antitrust and other governmental regulations.

Ethical dilemmas face the manager as he tries to meet all the commitments of the firm to employees, customers, stockholders, and the public.

The role of the corporation in society is expressed by Henry Ford II in an address entitled "Business Ethics in 1961."

> A corporation may be primarily a producer of goods, but it is more than just that; it is a small

society within society, one with motivations, with rules and principles of its own. It is a purposeful organization that can and must give more than just money to those who serve it, and those it serves. It should reflect in its daily actions the principles and aspiration of our society in its finest tradition.[2]

The corporation is in relationship with various claimants, which the manager through decision-making can satisfy or not satisfy. The following model illustrates these relationships:

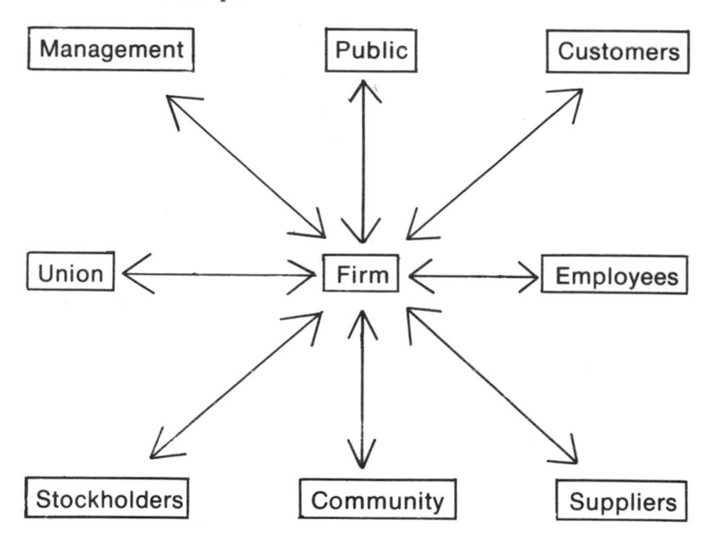


**Diagram 2**

The social-responsibility discussion in modern business arises from questions of how and in what way business will satisfy these various demands and behave in these relationships. Each of the groups illustrated in

Diagram 2 makes demands on the resources of the firm. The moral justification of their claims may be supported by tradition, law, social or personal values, or the government. The ethical problem confronting the manager is not only which demands shall be satisfied but also in what order of priority.

Business ethical problems in modern society arise from the social involvement of the firm. The issue is no longer whether business will be socially responsible, for it is already involved in the social and economic systems. The issues of business ethics relate to the way in which this social responsibility will be discharged and what ethical guidelines will be used in the modern business system.

The managers who exercise control and power in the organization are not the owners. Business ethics that relates solely to the exercise of private property and the right of contract does not deal with the total dimension of the modern manager's role and function in the corporation.

The organization is the center of focus and concern, since it is semiautonomous, self-perpetuating, and continuous.

The corporation exercises not only economic power but social power. It satisfies not only people's demands for money but their social needs in and through an organization.

The public welfare is pursued by government. As a participant in the economy the businessman has to face the social goals established by government, since these affect his operation and conduct.

The existence of unions and other competing power groups means that the businessman carries out his functions not in a perfect market structure but in a pluralistic economy, bargaining with other groups.

The stockholders are not those who control the organization and have the only claim on the firm. The ethics of management behavior includes much more than the stewardship of financial capital.

To meet the goals of the organization, the manager controls the total assets of the firm. These include employees, social reputation, product acceptance, and the character of the organization within a social and cultural environment, which his activities affect and which in turn affect him.

The businessman conducts his activities in a changing world of values, of preferences, and of goals, for which he requires appropriate business ethics.

BOAC
8
AC
RCA
PS
4
AP

# 3
# *Approaches to Business Ethics*

The need for ethics in business as in all human relationships has occupied the attention of many people. The approaches have ranged from those who would tinker with our current system to those who, like Karl Marx and the socialists, would destroy the present system and replace it with another. Although many view our present system as devoted to capital accumulation, profits, and labor exploitation and feel that only a new society or a different system would overcome our current business-ethical problems, I do not share this position. Approaches to business ethics that seek to improve the modern business system by establishing a new system fail all too often to recognize the merits of our current society and underestimate the weakness of people.

The approaches to business ethics that I think are realistic and useful are those that relate to our existing democratic, social, and economic structures.

### *Business Ethics and Economic Efficiency*

Some believe that bad business ethics consists of interferences with the perfectly competitive economic model and with profit-maximizing behavior. Variations from efficient production and from the most efficient distribution of income and allocation of resources are considered unethical. According to this view, business managers who interfere with the free market prevent the market from disciplining a firm's behavior, determining prices by market forces, and providing the "best" utilization of resources. The directive that business managers should engage in profit-maximizing behavior and face-to-face civility is based on a belief that competition, market forces, and self-interest will provide the greatest social welfare and the greatest amount of efficiency.

The economic model embodied in the theory of pure capitalism assumes private property, the right of contract, and work. Monopolies, whether in business or in labor, prevent wages from being equal to the value of the worker's product, keep prices from reflecting market forces, and prevent people from receiving the quantity of product that is their right in the marketplace. The monopolist, if he acts as a discriminatory monopolist, will charge what the traffic will bear. Injustices result as the businessman charges a higher price to the rich man than to the poor man for the same service, as labor monopolies use power to get higher wages, or as the manager is forced to pay a higher price for a product because there are no alternative sources of supply.

Ethics would be improved as one supports or returns to the economic model of perfect competition, which seems to answer questions of a "just price," "usury," a "just wage," or a "fair profit." Bad ethics is a conscious deviation from "perfect competition," since it results in social injustices.

John Bates Clark, using the perfect-competition model, could defend the existing wages of employees as just because they were equivalent to the value of their output. Wages could be increased only as laborers increased their work or as the price of the final product rose. The cost of production determined the cost of supply, the level of demand was determined by what people were prepared to pay for the product, so that the final price was a result of cost and demand meeting in a free market. The existing wage was the just wage.

This approach to business ethics requires the breaking up of monopolies, whether of business or labor, removing the interfering hand of government, and establishing a free market. Wages would then be proportional to the value of the output of the worker. Such an approach would remove the unethical practice of paying a man more than he produces, i. e., more than he is worth. Interest would then be related to the cost of inducing people to refrain from consumption, to the productivity of capital, and to a charge for the use of capital. The price in the market would be "ethical," for it would be directly equal to the amount people were willing to pay and at a price suppliers were willing to offer products.

This approach is useful if one assumes that there can be a free market, that managers have no influence on the level of prices, and that the decision-making process of managers will be based solely on competition. These assumptions, however, are unrealistic in our modern business system. The free-market ideal of the economist is a model of efficiency. *Ethics cannot be equated with efficiency, as is done in the classical economic model.* Efficiency is not a sufficient guide for good ethical practices. No end of confusion has resulted from a belief that simply because the economist can rationally establish and advise on the most efficient way to combine inputs this is the way things should be combined. It is precisely the "should" which is at issue in the problem of business ethics.

There is no general agreement that competition is the most efficient way to structure all human activity. The capitalistic ideal tends to ignore the ability of the manager and the government decision-makers to affect both the structure and the results. The existence of "imperfections" in the market have not led to injustices. The efforts of employees to combine together cannot be condemned ahead of time as unethical. Ethics is to be measured by results, not the structure. Not all activities of government have resulted in bad results, as not all activities of private business through competition have resulted in fair practices and justice.

*Business Ethics by Personal Morality*

Business ethics has been identified with moral behavior. As an individual lives his personal life by the Golden Rule, so in business he lives by the same standard. However, as James Culliton stated after having discussions of business behavior at a Danforth Foundation Seminar in 1957 at the Harvard Business School: "So by and large we ended up in favor of honesty and the Golden Rule." [1]

Business ethics as adherence to or deviation from the Ten Commandments has received support from Christian and non-Christian scholars. Rabbi David H. Panitz, in an article entitled "Business and Ethics in the Hebrew Tradition," spoke of the contribution of Judaism and gave the following advice to a business-policy class in the School of Business at Rutgers: "Your success in life, however, will be judged by the following criteria: Do you offer your fellow man the best possible and the most trustworthy product or service, do you treat all those around you with a profound concern for human values, and do you encourage others to raise social standards and to aspire towards the ideals of mankind?" [2]

In this view, business ethics can be improved by improving the morality of the people who conduct business. The application of personal moral standards will direct the behavior of businessmen as they observe honesty, truthfulness, and respect for other people and their property.

A successful businessman, Roy Oscarson, executive vice-president of Edison Brothers Stores, Inc., wrote: "Those whom we regard as truly successful have characterized their business and professional lives by keeping promises, giving full measure and value, accepting criticism, and forsaking deceitful practices." [3]

Ben Rogge, in a seminar on business and ethics sponsored by the Lutheran Academy for Scholarship, recognized the problem of business ethics as more than simply morality. At that seminar he proposed that economic ethics must be comprehended with these concepts: man is imperfect; man is a responsible being; man has the freedom to choose; man is part of the brotherhood of man. As an explicit guideline he added, "Thou shalt not steal." The question came back, But what do you mean by stealing?

John Hess seems to be pointing in the direction of business ethics as moral behavior. "Regardless of our role: laborer or employer, seller or buyer, producer or consumer, those who call themselves Christian must constantly ask themselves whether they are applying Christian teachings to all their transactions. Further, in viewing the actions of others we should follow Christ's admonition not to judge our brother hastily and uncharitably. . . . Sunday ethics, the Ten Commandments, and the Golden Rule definitely are translatable every day to the market place." [4]

The guidelines of personal morality as the way in which business plays the game of business leaves unanswered many significant questions. An accountant for the Mafia may be ever so honest, but is there not an ethical question of his employment with this group? A manager may be ever so truthful, but should he fire the 63-year-old employee who is no longer producing? The commandment "Thou shalt not kill" embraces matters of health, but does it embrace the use of potentially unsafe products and equipment?

Because the meaning of private property has undergone continual change in our society and as our business system has become so complex, one cannot answer all business-ethical questions by appeals to honesty and the Golden Rule. Is it stealing to build a glue factory across from my house so that the value of my property drops? Should businessmen engage in politics? Should one give to the Community Chest? Expansions of the meanings of killing, stealing, and lying are appropriate concerns of business ethics, but having answered these questions, many problems of justice and ethics in relationships between individuals and groups still remain.

One author has compared business to a game of poker, where bluffing is part of the game. Is the poker player who bluffs his hand to win the pot really acting unethically? Since the rules of the game are known by all the participants, others expect and anticipate bluffing; and being forewarned, they are not deceived. If all those who are involved in the business system understand the rules of the game, they should anticipate and be prepared for certain types of behavior. The issue of morality in business ethics, then, is the problem of making clear the rules ahead of time.

The appeal of business ethics as personal morality is that one can defend both private property and private contracts. An honest day's work for an honest day's pay sounds fair, just, and reasonable. Profit is reward for honest effort, as is also the receipt of interest. One can defend attacks on property by appeals to the Ten Commandments. The personal-morality approach places business ethics on a standard of morality with which most people would agree.

*Business Ethics and Capitalism*

Business ethics has been identified with a defense of the economic system of capitalism on the grounds that the capitalistic economic system is that which is also the most ethical.

The capitalistic system allows free choice and opportunity. In contrast, the socialist system operates with central planning and central direction. Ethical businessmen defend free enterprise, unethical businessmen seek to destroy it. Business ethics consists of preserving the system that has provided great material abundance simultaneously with great freedom. Business ethics consists of providing the greatest material abundance as measured by gross national product and of supporting the system that does this well within an environment of freedom.

Theodore Y. Yntema in the Benjamin Fairless Memorial Lectures of 1964, entitled *The Enrichment of Man,* defended this approach. As he drew an analogy between capitalism and socialism, he defended the capitalist system not only because it provided enrichment of men but also because it was the most efficient and supported the common good through pursuing one's self-interest. "This economy of ours not only employs the acquisitive drives to serve the social interest; it also provides opportunity for the exercise of the nobler virtues—for charity and good works. But if we try to accomplish everything by altruism there won't be enough altruism to go around. . . . The private enterprise system transmutes the selfish drives of men into service of others —and does it with a high yield."[5]

The capitalist system is built on freedom and opportunities. Anything that interferes with freedom and opportunity, or initiative, is to be opposed as unethical.

The adoption by businessmen of a social responsibility directed to the alleviation of the ills and problems in society has been rejected for the very reason that it interferes with the freedom of the individual either by changing the structure of our pluralistic society or by taking actions on which a consensus has not been secured. Social responsibility would require that businessmen make decisions about social conditions, social welfare, and the interests of consumers. Theodore Levitt declares that this would lead to a new feudalism. "It is the function of business to produce sustained high-level profits,"[6] not to care for the social welfare. Social responsibility as a guide to business behavior would lead to a monolithic society, socialism, and a fusion of social power of the corporation with the political power of the state. Levitt further asserts: "Altruism, self-denial, charity, and similar values are vital in certain walks of our life —areas which, because of that fact, are more important to the long-run future of business. But for the most part those virtues are alien to competitive economics."[7]

Capitalism, it is said, is the working structure of the free-enterprise system with which we are familiar. It is built on well-known responsibilities and functions. Businessmen, many say, are beyond their depth when they try to perform the social welfare work that should be done by the church and others.

The business ethics of capitalism is related to

a belief in the Protestant ethic. The logical deduction of the relationship is often made. Capitalism supports the importance of the individual; so does Christianity. Capitalism protects the use of and holding private property; so do the Ten Commandments. Capitalism places the responsibility of choice on the individual; so does Christianity. Capitalism rewards morality, thrift, hard work, industriousness; Christianity does not ignore the relationship between good works and final rewards. To oppose capitalism is to oppose Christianity. As one writer has put the issue: "Because the free enterprise system produces greater economic progress than would be possible under any other economic system known at the present, it is doing more to advance the broader goals of Christianity than could any other existing arrangement." [8]

The code of ethics of the National Association of Manufacturers, mentioned earlier, tries to relate the two. Their concern is with the preservation of a system and a society in which ethical concerns include the protection of private property and the right of contract.

The relationship of capitalism to democracy should not be ignored. Democracy as it has been understood is built on the behavior of responsible, independent people. As he guards economic freedom, the businessman also is protecting political freedom. There is no doubt that capitalism has made it possible for the church to enjoy relative freedom and that many of the values of Christianity are present in the capitalist structure. Business ethics, however, is something more than equating Christianity with a capitalist structure or with any other economic or business structure.

*Business Ethics and Management Codes*

The complexity of modern business, the expansion of the corporation, and the rise of management have created a need for different kinds of guides for ethical behavior. The ethical guidelines of capitalism and the free-market economy are deficient because management now operates in a mixed economy and many of its decisions relate to organizational matters and the behavior of the firm in our modern society. Managers are often not involved in great economic questions of free markets or capitalism but with the ordinary functions of operating a business.

The need for providing ethical guidelines for managers has led to the writing of management codes or creeds.

The American Management Association in *Management Creeds and Philosophies* reported that company creeds have been set up to define the purpose of the company; to clarify the philosophy character of the company; to create a particular "climate within the business, and to set down guides for managers." The company creed was really the "most basic sort of guiding statement of company objectives which also lays down the ethical practices to be adhered to in achieving these objectives." [9] In many cases creeds extend beyond an adherence to private property and honesty and try to provide ethical guidelines for policy and action.

The creed of General Motors includes six principles:

1. Put the right people in the right place. . . .
2. Train everyone for the job to be done. . . .
3. Make the organization a coordinated team. . . .
4. Supply the right tools and the right conditions. . . .
5. Give security with opportunity, incentive, recognition. . . .

> 6. Look ahead, plan ahead for more and better things. Following and developing these principles will help us to accomplish our objectives and enable General Motors to produce "More and better things for more people." [10]

The creed of Eriez Manufacturing Company of Erie, Pa., recognizes that business owes a responsibility broader than that of simply good business practices.

> Using the Golden Rule as a guide—to build an organization that will give our associates the best possible job opportunity, work satisfactions, happiness and security; our customers a higher quality product at a favorable price commensurate with good service before and after sale; our stockholders a reasonable continuing return on their investment—and conduct our affairs in such an efficient, capable, and friendly manner that everyone who comes in contact with us would be happy to be one associated with us.[11]

The success of the creeds in improving business ethical practices seems to be mixed. Creeds which an individual created for himself seem to be of more value than those written by others. Not all management people accepted, used, or even knew of the creeds in the company.

Management creeds are important because they recognize that business ethics includes more than personal moral standards for managers; it includes placement of people, providing satisfactions to associates, security, and some commitment to the welfare of society.

*Business Ethics by Legislation*

The state of business ethics both in the present and in the past has not been ignored by government. The muckrakers pointed to the abuses in the oil industry

(Ida Tarbell's *History of the Standard Oil Company of New Jersey*) and in the meat-packing industry (Upton Sinclair's *The Jungle*) and argued for government action to correct the abuses. Prior to their disclosures the government had passed the Sherman Anti-Trust Act (1890), which was directed at pools and combinations in restraint of trade.

Government agencies concerned with correcting business practices include: food and drugs—Food and Drug Administration; weights and standards—Bureau of Weights and Standards, Department of Commerce; restraint of trade—Anti-Trust Division of the Justice Department; consumer products—Director of Consumer Affairs, Office of the President; labor relations—Department of Labor.

Legislation of various kinds has been directed against what are believed to be bad business practices, whether in products or practices. Automobile-safety legislation has joined the truth-in-packaging legislation in trying to secure better products.

The application of standards by legislation has been motivated in the consumer area by a belief that business would not correct itself, a rising tide of what is called "consumerism," and a desire to secure justice and safety. Underlying much legislation are the assumptions that the consumer is unable to choose what is best for him, self-regulation by business is ineffective, and it is government's responsibility to control and direct the exercise of power. There are strong feelings that the consumer is unable to control the activities of business firms and the quality of their products. Government legislation has arisen from a recognition that our economic system is not so perfect that we can rely on the free market, consumer sovereignty, and the knowledge of the consumer to create good business practices.

The thought of Martin Luther seems to have been answered when he wrote: "Therefore the world needs a strict, hard temporal government that will compel and constrain the wicked not to steal and rob and to return what they borrow, even though a Christian ought not demand it, or even hope to get it back. This is necessary in order that the world may not become a desert, peace may not perish, and trade and society may not be utterly destroyed." [12]

*Business Ethics by Professional Standards*

The increasing importance of management to the operation of modern business has caused many to insist that management is a science and its practice is a profession. Business ethics can be improved by the development of standards of professional ethics. Since the manager establishes ethical practices in business, he needs a standard of professional ethics similar to those in law, theology, or medicine.

A profession requires a certain core of knowledge —intellectually acquired; a relationship of responsibility to clients; and responsible associations that set standards of admission and enforce a code of ethics.

There is no general agreement that management has or can ever have all these prerequisites. In our economic system any person regardless of his training can engage in business for himself or as an employee. The artist who sells pictures, the part-time magazine saleswoman who is also a housewife, and the clergyman who looks after a bookrack in the church are engaging in business.

In the large organization and the corporation one can speak of professionalization in the way that Joseph W. Towle and others do in *Ethics and Standards in American*

*Business*. Towle points to the development of professional schools of business administration, to professional management societies and associations, and to business-ethics advisory councils as evidences of a trend toward professionalization of business.

Business ethics will be improved with the development of such organizations as the Certified Accountants Association, which establishes ethical standards. The same is true of the Certified Life Underwriters. Towle concludes by insisting: "The search by business executives for a 'better way' and a moral philosophy will contribute to the emergence of management as a profession." [13]

How does one get professionalization of business? Does one first make management a profession, then agree on codes? Or does one establish a moral philosophy first, and by this essential ingredient create a profession?

The success of the improvement of ethics by professional standards will depend on the development of a uniform science and knowledge by which one can eliminate those who ought not be in the management profession.

The development of management as a profession would certainly eliminate many of the evil men in business, but the real question remains whether it would do much more than establish a method by which standards of personal conduct could be improved. It may do much to improve the moral climate of the performance of one's functions, that is, to secure honesty, uprightness, quality of product, good management and employee relationships, and contribute to the moral philosophy of business.

### *Business Ethics as Social Responsibility*

As a significant social and economic force in our economy, business possesses the ability and the power to accomplish or hinder social goals as well as determine the structure of our society. Questions of how the social and economic power of the corporation will be used provide other dimensions to the problem of business ethics. The approach to business ethics through the social behavior of the firm is social responsibility.

The view that business ethics must include socially responsible behavior arises from a belief that social responsibility must be equal to social power. Business creates jobs or reduces them; it improves our living areas or destroys them; it gives us products, whether useful or destructive; it provides us with opportunities for self-development or destroys the self in the organization; it gives us occasions for charity or assists in making life selfish; and it does encourage or discourage the order by which we live in community. The power and pervasiveness of business no longer raises the question of whether business will affect our society but only how it will do so.

Social responsibility as a dimension of ethical concern is supported by James Worthy, former assistant undersecretary of commerce: "Professional managers are coming to recognize that business can no longer pursue its economic interests regardless of social consequences." [14]

In 1966 *Newsweek* reported on a survey that showed that large majorities of people want business to assume leadership in broad social areas. The response indicated that people believe that business ought to accept ethical and social responsibilities in these areas: [15]

| | % AGREE |
|---|---|
| Eliminating depressions | 92 |
| Rebuilding cities | 87 |
| Finding cures for disease | 72 |

| | |
|---|---|
| Aiding college education | 83 |
| Wiping out poverty | 80 |
| Eliminating racial prejudice | 83 |
| Controlling pollution | 90 |

A guideline for business in its social responsibilities has come from the concept of a good corporate citizen. The good citizen in a country performs deeds of charity and compassion, contributes to education, supports social betterment, and lives at peace with his neighbors. Obedience to the law and moral and physical support of all aspects of social betterment are essential ingredients of the practice of good citizenship. The view that good corporate ethics is equivalent to good citizenship ethics has gained wide favor.

The search for guidelines for socially responsible behavior has caused business to support the things that government accepts by legislation or policy statement as being socially desirable. A business acts responsibly as it contributes to education, cooperates with the government in employing and training those in the slums, cleans up air pollution and water pollution, and makes factories pleasant and esthetically beautiful. The government has contributed to underdeveloped countries as an expression of social and humanitarian concerns. Many believe that business is acting ethically as it too builds factories, loans capital, and provides technical and management assistance to raise the standard of living of other countries.

Business is believed to be acting in a socially responsible manner as it participates with the government in what Max Ways calls a new federalism. The manager is acting ethically when he accepts the role of the firm in society as a social resource to be used in cooperation with the government in meeting the discovered needs of society in many ways and on many fronts.

# 4

# *Christian Perspectives on Business Ethics*

The Christian in business does not employ a different ethical standard from that used by the Christian in any other place, but his ethical concerns are meant to be related to action in the business and economic system. Denys L. Munby has pointed out that the New Testament is of little use as a manual of conduct. The ethical imperative our Lord provided His disciples, "that ye love one another as I have loved you," cannot be commanded. Christian love is meant to describe the kind of people we ought to be and is limited as a guide for behavior in the business world.

Christian ethics in a world of business originates in the relationship of faith, which directs the Christian to approach the world as a creation of God and to see this world as a place for service.

### *The Christian's Vocation*

Business ethics is based on Christian vocation. The Protestant ethic, as expressed in the Reformed tradition, equated predestination with one's earthly calling. The Christian was to perceive his earthly calling as something to which God had called him to service in this special time and special place.

In the New Testament, vocation involves one's relationship to Christ and to the church. Through the work of the Holy Spirit God calls men into the fellowship of the holy people of God, the church, the communion of saints. St. Paul writes to Timothy: "[God has] saved us and called us with a holy calling, not in virtue of our works but in virtue of His own purpose and the grace which He gave us in Christ Jesus" (2 Timothy 1:9). Our Lord reminded His disciples: "You did not choose Me, but I chose you and appointed you" (John 15:16). The Third Article of the Creed reminds us that "the Holy Ghost has called us through the Gospel."

The question is, however, whether God calls men into various secular occupations. This is not clearly stated in the Scriptures. The principal reference is 1 Corinthians 7:17-24, especially verse 20: "Everyone should remain in the state in which he was called." The Greek word *klesis* refers to the status or station in this world in which he found himself when he was called. This verse does not equate an avocation (one's work) with a calling of God. God does not call people to be plumbers, businessmen, lawyers or doctors. One cannot understand one's role as a businessman as a direct call from God. The call to be a Christian is found in whatever state a person finds himself (cf. 1 Corinthians 7:24).

Luther, in his sermon "On Keeping Children in School," wrote that "the spiritual estate has been established and instituted by God." The ministry is the most important estate, as the church indicates by her system of extending official calls to pastors and teachers. The vocation of a special calling is to some area of special service within the church. Luther felt that the office of worldly government was not comparable to the spiritual office of preaching; but it was a creation and ordinance of God. The analogy is appropriate for the businessman.

Luther's view of vocation was to perceive man's life as comparable to two sides of a coin. Man's earthly life and his occupation is a vocation, a part of the order of creation, while his spiritual calling arises from God's work of redemption. Man is called in the kingdom of creation (the world) to a life of service to his fellowmen, and in the kingdom of grace (the church) to a life of forgiveness, faith, and godly living.

This two-sided concept of vocation establishes occupations and the Christian's work in this world as service in the order of creation. Man fulfills a role in creation under the control of God, but from necessity and the need to care for the physical needs of men.

Nothing could be worse for the cause of Christianity than to equate one's occupation in this world with God's special calling or His act of predestination. To do so would be to accept every occupation as originating in the spiritual calling of God.

As part of creation and as part of his special calling to be a Christian a person is under the direct concern of God. As the work of creation and redemption both belong to the same God, so does a person's life within the church and in this world. Vocation, in this Christian sense, includes all that man is—not one special part.

A Christian sees his total vocation, whether as father or mother, son or daughter, businessman or legislator, as a means and an opportunity for service. Because one cannot refer to one's occupation as a divine calling does not demean it. One cannot separate one's avocation from his vocation. It means only that he is part of two worlds. In the kingdom of grace, love applies; in the kingdom of the world, law applies.

The social, economic, and political structures owe their origin to God. Luther in developing his concept of a Christian's "vocation of service in the world" affirmed six basic theses:

(a) Every Christian has a vocation in the world because every Christian has a station in which he can serve his fellows. (b) Vocation in the world is given structure by means of divinely established orders and offices. (c) Everything a Christian does in his vocation in the world is for the sake of human welfare. (d) All service in vocation ranks the same with God but not all offices have the same significance in society. (e) A Christian should be grateful that he has a God-given vocation where he can remain in loving service. (f) All young persons should have opportunity to prepare for the offices for which they are best qualified.[1]

*The Doctrine of Work*

Work has been considered by some as a punishment of God for man's sinfulness. This view is rooted in the Old Testament account of man's disobedience in the Garden of Eden, in consequence of which God imposes on man work with pain, sorrow, and suffering. (Genesis 3:17-19)

St. Paul also asserts to the Thessalonians that God ordained work for all. Although the concept of punishment is absent, his directions are clear: "If anyone will not work, let him not eat." (2 Thessalonians 3:10)

Work did not originate with sinfulness and God's punishment. God gave directions to man in the Garden of Eden: "Be fruitful and multiply and fill the earth and subdue it" (Genesis 1:27). He was to till the garden and keep it (2:15). The fall of man changed the character of work from a joy to a necessary struggle.

In the New Testament, work is considered a service performed by the redeemed Christian. St. Paul was writing to instruct the freeloading people at Thessalonica who were waiting for the second coming of Christ. He defended his own labor as necessary to spare his congregations from supporting him as he fulfilled his ministry. The people at Thessalonica were trying to live as if Christ's second coming was assuredly only hours or days away.

Within the social structure or the economic system, as a slave (as Paul wrote to Philemon) or as a businessman, one needs to carry out the vocation of being a Christian. One cannot carry on his vocation within the creation of God without activity.

Work presupposes that there is a world in which man can apply his creative activity. The direction to work is not a curse but a recognition that a man is compelled to carry out some creative activity in this world. As one fulfills his obligation of service to his fellowmen and thus to God, he will do this through the structures, systems, and economic order God has given. St. Paul repeatedly pointed out that God's power and will are expressed in the world of creation as well as in the church. God calls men and commands men to some kind of creative servant activity in relationship to His created world.

Rufus Cornelsen seems to have caught the spirit of work in the light of the New Testament when he writes: "Therefore, whereas animals are submerged in the world, man confronts the world. . . . In human activity instinct is interrupted by the deliberation of the self and the decision of the will. This conscientious, deliberative, decisional character of human action qualifies man's economic activity as work. It is a godlike endowment."[2]

The nature of a Christian's activity, as Luther recognized, is determined by the orders of creation, or the structure of the system in which one finds himself. Work provides man with opportunity. The capacity and competence for activity in this world is an opportunity for the Christian. Through work he is given an opportunity to serve his fellowmen, seek justice in God's creation, and express his calling as a Christian. The Christian is not driven to work; he seeks it.

The Christian does not fulfill his obligation of service to his fellowmen simply by working. One's obligations are not fulfilled once an assigned task has been completed or a particular job accomplished. The laying of bricks, the wiring of a house, the counting of money can be seen simply as a job. The Christian uses the knowledge of his job as an opportunity for service and for applying the creative hand of his calling.

Given the structure of our society, he who does not work will not have the means to perform deeds of charity or acts of love. In the economic structure of our society, unless a person participates in the working world, he is unable to accomplish love, change the structure of our society, or bring about a sense of community.

*The Christian and Competence*

The faith a Christian brings to the work or occupations of this world is not a substitute for technical competence. The Christian businessman is not spared knowledge of markets, demand and supply, labor relations, or technical competence simply because he is a Christian.

The call to service demands that one's service in the orders of creation will require a person to be a competent businessman and an aware member of the community. One can serve effectively only if he possesses the skill and competence necessary to perform enlightened and competent service to the world.

The Christian perceives the abilities God has given him as something to be developed, expanded, and used in the spirit of service. His motivation is not the earning of salvation; that is a gift of God through grace. The development of his abilities is related to his opportunities for service to his fellowmen and to the creation of God. The untrained, incompetent man is limited in his capacity to serve and in his knowledge of opportunities. The stewardship of life and of possessions involves responsibilities to use to the fullest what God has given a person, as the parables of the talents illustrate.

The Christian, as he subjects all his abilities, competence, money, and property to the service of mankind, is motivated by thankfulness to God. Faith guides him into the place of service as he reenacts the mercy and compassion of Christ in this world.

Competence and abilities in this world are a form of power over and in the world. For most people education, by which our gifts are developed, is often access to the power of this world. Only through competence and skill can a person participate in the work of the world and work with others of like skill in the accomplishment of justice.

Christian stewardship directs a Christian to the utilization of abilities, materials, and power that he controls, and it provides a goal for their use. The doctrine of work leads the Christian to competent management and activity related to the creation of God. Christian ethics provides him with the way these things and these relationships are to be conducted.

*Christian Ethics*

The Christian man, as Joseph Sittler points out, accepts what God gives as the Creator. This means the world, with its needs, problems, and possibilities. Within this world he is to operate as a redeemed man, exercising love with directions provided by his faith. As the Christian perceives this world as God's creation, the Ten Commandments take on a different orientation. Sittler writes that the Ten Commandments are "disclosures of the Creator-creature structure of existence . . . of the requirements that inhere in the human situation simply by virtue of its source in God and the structure which he has given it."[3]

The Ten Commandments are evidences of the basic structure that God desires and wills should be maintained within the order of creation—two sexes, marriage, and family, for example. The things that man has made for his life and support, such as property, government, and the economic system, are also to be respected.

The Ten Commandments as expressions of the will of God provide a foundation for a God-given structure to the creative world. The relationships between men are meant to be structured on the Ten Commandments, which command, for example, honesty, preservation of the property one owns or controls, and fidelity in marriage.

What does the Christian try to bring to the creation of God? The answer is justice. The need here, as Jaroslav Pelikan points out, is for prudence and fortitude. The advice he gives to Christian lawyers is equally applicable to the Christian businessman: "The Christian lawyer is free to do what he can do, and he is willing to do what he must do; for he lives by the gift of *justitia* as righteousness and lives for the goal of *justitia* as justice. He can collaborate with all those who aim for this goal, regardless of their relation to *justitia* as righteousness, believers or not, because he knows that the laws and structures of society 'are actually good and useful, but in the proper order and proper place.'"[4]

The Christian as a realist moves society from its present condition to the ultimate goal by taking one step at a time.

The Ten Commandments structure man's relationships in creation to secure justice and to form the basis for community. One's relationship to his fellowmen is comprehended in the concept that God not only wills certain actions for people but that man lives in community and in justice.

There is no distinction between personal ethics and social ethics. Both are related to a man's performance within community and are for the creation of justice in community with one another. The Christian is concerned about personal ethics, but he cannot avoid an equal concern for social ethics. The involvement of the Christian in the social sphere requires him to try to establish justice. He recognizes, however, that justice can never be established in the same way that justice as the righteousness of God is present within the kingdom of God. Christian ethics is given content as he selects alternatives to serve the common good and to establish justice in the community of men.

Private property is not an absolute right within the Christian meaning of service to one's neighbor. Stewardship sees all property, whether owned or controlled, as that which is readily available to the service of one's fellowmen. The defense of private property is rooted in the need to preserve order in creation. Community is preserved as a person has protection in the use of life and property and the occasion to use this to accomplish the goals he seeks. Property is held as a trust from God; it is owned by God, and it is always to be used in reference to the creation and maintenance of community.

Christian ethics calls the Christian to serve with *all* that he has. Adolph Köberle writes: "Because the distress of external circumstances, as well as the evils within, can obstruct the way to God, a faith that is prepared to help must address itself to the whole man in his actual condition and must offer to help with both hands; the Word with the right hand and love with the left. It must bring forgiveness *and* fellowship, the physician *and* the remedy, the bread of life *and* daily bread." [5]

Christian ethics is concerned with justice while providing the creaturely needs and creating community among men. The Christian consequently can cooperate with other non-Christians in creating civil righteousness, building just relationships, and satisfying people's basic needs.

The meaning of a kingdom of love and of human relationships with one another is revealed in the Sermon on the Mount. This does not consist of guides for ethical behavior. Our Lord was not laying down new rules, laws, and regulations. He provided an image, a picture, a paradigm of what God means by a community of love in its perfection, a spirit of Christian concern, and the righteousness of God in this world. The Sermon on the Mount exhibits the meaning of love as expressed in a community of service and obedience.

Christ does not provide us with Christian principles for the ordering of human community. Faith in Christ leads us to activity and to the kind of responses we are to take in this world. Faith reminds us that we are creatures and also that through faith we learn to differentiate between facts and act on them. Through faith we learn of the dignity of man, the value of the human being, and the worth of an individual in the sight of God.

*The Tools of Christian Concern*

The accomplishment of justice in human relationships and in community demands Christian involvement in the institutions, organizations, and structures that are part of the creation of God. Although there can be justice in society without reference to God, the Christian's concern and passion for justice arises from his relationship to God. Luther reminds us that human institutions are the masks of God, behind which He acts and reveals His will. The concern for community involves participation in the things by which community is furthered, fostered, and established. The creation of social justice in the political realm involves the participation and utilization of the means by which political freedom and justice is secured—political parties, kissing babies, legislative caucuses, pressure groups, and so on.

The same is true of the economic sphere. The corporation as an instrument of economic production in our economy is a human structure and form for the creation of output and satisfactions of people. It is amoral rather than immoral. Howard R. Bowen expressed the interdependence of all economic life thus:

> To summarize, economic life in all its ramifications is of profound ethical significance. This is so because of scarcity which gives rise to conflict, because of interdependence which creates mutual obligations, because of the wide range of values sought through economic activity, and because of the significance for human life of the economic process itself.[6]

Ethics is expressed by the use of power, which may be social, economic, or political. The Christian uses whatever means he has to express love for his fellowmen.

Some have taken the words of the Sermon on the Mount, "Take no thought for the morrow," to mean that one should oppose insurance, social security, pension plans, and other human arrangements for the protection of people in old age, sickness, and disease. The Gospel does not limit man's activities to employ the structures of creation for the accomplishment of the protection of life, safety, and his own welfare.

A 1946 statement of principles adopted by the Executive Board and the Board of Social Missions of the United Lutheran Church of America stated among other things:

> It is the right of every man to receive a wage commensurate with his abilities, and, wherever feasible, in cooperation with his co-workers, to share in the direction and management of his labors. . . .
>
> It is the duty of every man to provide adequate living for himself and his dependents. . . .
>
> It is the right of every man freely to set up and to maintain, in cooperation with his fellowmen, such forms of health and accident insurance, provision for medical care, unemployment relief and insurance, and old age pensions as will provide security against the hazards of life. It is the right of every man to organize with his fellow workers for collective bargaining through representatives of his own free choice.[7]

As he uses the structures, institutions, and methods for the maintenance, accomplishment, and securing of justice, the Christian knows that he can bring only justice, never perfect love. He can work within the context of limited objectives. The good that a Christian brings is destroyed and requires restoration. The objectives are not total justice but justice in areas or sections or practices.

NEW YORK

# 5

# Christian Ethics and Business Ethics

The Christian in business makes ethical decisions as he is faced with imperfect alternatives on all sides. He is able to implement only incomplete justice and imperfect order. In this tension he acts not with a set of principles but with faith, a love for mankind, a willingness to serve, and a passion for justice.

As the Christian businessman seeks justice and fulfills his vocation, there are three dimensions to his ethical concerns:

a) ethics relating to his job and its practices;
b) ethics of his relationships within the business organization; and
c) ethics of his management of the organization within the structure of society and within community.

The businessman is part of the total social system and community within which he operates. The manager carries on his activities in a social system (the organization) and with and through social structures (the community). The dimensions of his ethical concerns must include the total community in which he conducts his activities. Business ethics concerned only with the management of property and directed to economic criteria are too limited for the manager in the modern business system.

The view that the businessman should become socially responsible does not ignore the economic dimensions of life but rather insists that economics does not comprehend and determine all social goals. Economics may well establish limitations, but it should not determine activities. Economics tells us what we can do, not what we should do. An economic determinism that establishes goals and decides the things we should do is antithetical to the view that the economic society is created for man, not man for economic society.

The Christian businessman uses his ability, competence, power, and control over all resources, both social and economic, to serve mankind. His service does not ignore the economic relationships—people must work to receive income, pay for the goods and services they want, produce output in order to have goods and services, or contribute taxes to control inflation. The business functions must be carried on in the totality of man's needs and requirements, his desire to have justice in all his relationships, and his sense of community in all his activities.

The Christian businessman will adhere to the highest standards of personal integrity and conduct, honesty in relationships and practices, and a Christian sense of vocation.

The Christian businessman is part of society and its complexity and its tensions. His ethical concerns change because he cannot carry on his economic activities oblivious of and in ignorance of the standards of behavior that people have adopted to secure justice in their social relationships. The arrangements people have established to seek their goals, express their preferences, and secure the things they want cannot be ignored. The totality of man includes his social, legal, and political structures. The social setting of the business firm requires that the ethics of the business manager be more comprehensive than ethics related to a capitalist economy or the stewardship of financial resources.

*The Nature of Ethical Questions in Business and Society*

The involvement of the business firm and the manager with and in society requires a structuring of the relationships that exist between business and its environment. The following diagram is illustrative of the relationships of the business firm in its total social setting:

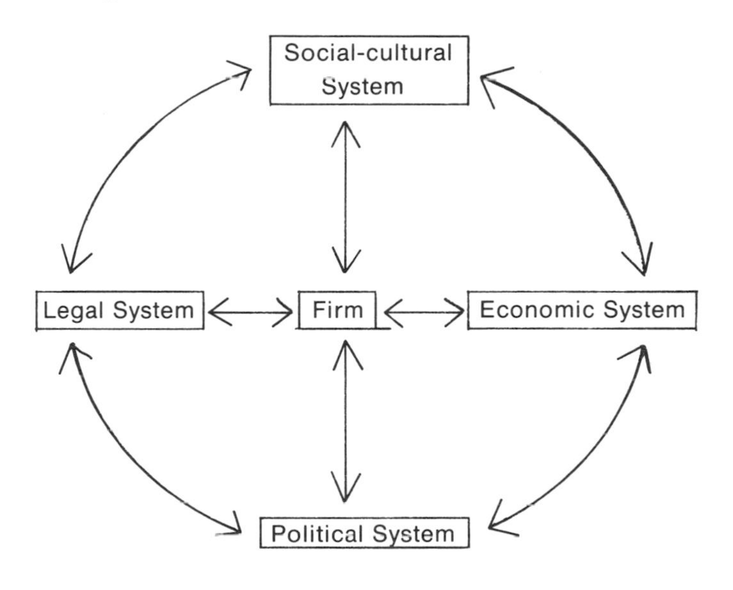


**Diagram 3**

The business firm interacts not with society in the abstract but with clearly identifiable parts—the legal system, the political system, the social-cultural system, and the economic system. Each part has its own goals and functions, which interact with each other and with the business firm.

The manager integrates these systems on the basis of his knowledge of their structures and goals. The relationships he has with these systems and the way he carries on his functions can be characterized as transactions, communications, transformations, organizations, and decision-making. The ethical tensions confronting him arise from the character and nature of these relationships and of the relationships that exist within the various systems.

Ethical questions arise for the manager as he seeks the goals of the business firm and makes decisions. His activities are always complex in nature because he becomes involved with the systems of society in varying degrees. The complexity of his activities can be reduced by examining the character of his relationships with the various systems.

The manager does not deal only with the economic system or only with economic matters. The nature of his activity means that he is exchanging goods, services, and other things for money, as well as money for goods, services, and other things. Money does not all flow in to the manager; some flows out in the form of wages, salaries, dividends, gifts, grants, and taxes. The manager engages in transactions—he exchanges goods and services for money; he bargains wages for work; he exchanges wage increases for labor peace; he provides social prestige and status in the organization in exchange for work performance; and he bargains social desires for benefits the organization can provide.

Many of these transactions are not undertaken in a market but are conducted within or outside the organization: with customers, the government, employees, fellow managers, and people. The economic marketplace is only one place where transactions are carried on. Since he is engaging in bargaining, the nature of transactions broadens the manager's ethical concerns rather than limits them.

The manager may bargain selfishly, that is, goods or services for money, favors, or advantages; or he may bargain generously, that is, giving gifts. At the heart of all bargaining is the use of power. Money is power in the economic sphere; prestige and status are power in society; the best legal talent is power in court; and knowledge is power in many areas.

The manager communicates with employees, the community, other businessmen, and customers—both actual and potential. Through speeches, advertising, public relations, newsletters, word of mouth, and the imparting of information, the manager tries to accomplish the goals of the firm. He directs people's behavior, scolds, praises, admonishes, and rewards through words, actions, and signs.

The firm, as an organization, and the manager, as an individual, engage in transformations or changes of structure, products, and the way in which the manager thinks. The firm may decide to expand in size, to employ more people, or to shrink the number of employees or product lines. These actions and activities are carried on by the manager as he makes decisions about the survival of the firm and the structure of the organization.

The manager accomplishes his goals as he works through organizations in addition to his own. He may deal with the government, unions, social groups, and other business organizations. The relationship with other organizations is often that of power to power.

The actions and activities of the organization are carried on as the manager makes decisions to move the firm through time, to structure the organization, to transform and market its products, and to deal with other organizations. Behind every action of the firm lies the decision-making manager who weighs values of different kinds, selects goals, engages in strategies or tactics, and accomplishes the functions of business.

The kinds of ethical decisions the manager faces originate in the nature of the relationships of the firm with the various systems and the character of the management function itself. Business ethics must include the ethics of the use of power, which the manager expresses in transactions, the use of communications, the seeking of goals in and through organizations, and the changing form of his own organization and ideas. The manager also faces ethical questions because he carries on activities not as an individual but as a representative of the organization. The manager selects goals, makes decisions, and chooses alternatives alone and in consultation with the other representatives of the firm. His decisions affect the institutional structure and the social system as well as the kinds and quantity of products that people have available. The nature of the manager's ethical problems arises from how and in what way he conducts his activities and the relationships with the environment of the firm and within the firm itself.

### *The Ethics of the Management Function*

The Christian manager fulfills his vocation as part of the organization and in a role within the organization. The individual working alone, in his avocation, fulfills the ethics of an artisan, as there is a direct relationship between his output and himself.

The ethical responsibility of the manager is to seek justice in his role and relationships within and outside the firm. He will seek to establish justice in transactions, communications, organizations, and transformations. Each of the various systems, however, holds values and concepts of what is just and fair. The manager not only seeks to uplift the current views of justice but also to uphold and support the highest standards of justice already accepted in the other systems. He follows and upholds the norms for legal activities as established in the legal system. He adheres to the rules of how to enter into contracts, establish prices, compete with other firms, determine the rate of interest, and deal justly with people.

The manager will employ the norms of the political system by which power is legitimized. Justice in our pluralistic society means the acceptance of alternate power groups as a way of controlling power. The union represents such a power bloc. It is unethical for the manager to seek to destroy the union. The political process operates to establish socially desirable values and goals such as water- and air-pollution control, social security systems, and income tax contributions based on a progressive rate. The values and goals of society must be shared by the manager.

The social and cultural system also holds values and norms of justice. The church as an organization is concerned with preserving the family, social justice, the integrity and value of the individual, and the freedom of church and state. The manager recognizes and operates within these values as well as other values of society, such as the importance of patriotism, the value of education, the significance of music, art, and literature in the culture of our society, and the importance of freedom of worship.

The manager acts ethically when in the social organization of the firm he seeks to uphold as a minimum what people believe is just, fair, and valuable. As a minimal condition one expects that business, as part of the community, needs to subordinate its own single-minded concern for profit maximization to the interests of the creation and maintenance of community and justice.

It would be unethical for the manager to refuse to hire Negroes, to deprive a person of his constitutional rights, to refuse to observe the due process of law, to produce a product designed to destroy the family, to refuse to obey water- and air-pollution laws, to try to destroy a union, or to market a product known to be illegal.

The ethics of the manager as he seeks justice involves the support of activities and structures through which it is possible for people to choose what they want and to change the meaning of justice. The ethical responsibility of the manager is not only to seek justice but also to preserve the process and ways by which justice is established. There is a place for the manager as a member of society and in various roles to change the values of society, to institute what he thinks is just and fair in the social, legal, and political systems. The Christian businessman should insist that it is the function of business to respond to the social needs of society, not to create them. It is not the role of business to create values, to determine social goals, to use its power irresponsibly, but rather to serve by producing goods and services and by satisfying the social wants of people working in the organization.

Each person who is part of the firm needs to perform activities that are determined by his job in order that the organization may survive. The firm as a system can exist only as each part of it maintains its relationships with each other part. The manager's role is to direct the functions of people to accomplish the goals of the firm and to perform his own job well.

As the manager directs and controls the functions of people, he views the organization as existing for the benefit of society. People do not exist for the firm. The firm contributes to the welfare of society through the performance of its economic and social functions.

The view of the firm as performing particular functions in society as part of the total system of society leads the manager to activities that maintain the total system. He conducts his job in the structures and systems of society and lives at peace with other systems. The limits of his role are defined by the functions of the firm in relationship to the other systems. Justice is secured as the manager does not exceed his functions, as the firm performs its proper role, and as the structures and forms of the other systems are maintained.

The Christian manager's ethical considerations will lead him to perform his functions with the following guidelines:

1. The manager acts ethically when he seeks to maintain, support, and continue the firm as an organization and as an operating unit. Only as the firm exists can it provide goods and services, social satisfactions for people, and contributions to the social and public welfare.

2. The manager acts ethically when he sees the organization as a means to an end but not an end in itself. The firm is not the goal, but rather the things produced by the firm. The organization exists to perform its functions.

3. The manager acts ethically when he exercises power to accomplish the goals of the firm within the norms of justice accepted in the social, political, legal, and economic framework. The firm provides not only work but also opportunity for the maintenance of life, health, and safety.

4. The manager acts ethically when he is concerned with efficiency of the firm's operations so that

the resources of creation can be effectively utilized and maximum use made of the limited resources of land, labor, capital, and managerial ability. A measure of the firm's efficiency and ability to survive is profit.

5. The manager acts ethically when he resists the use of the firm's social, economic, or political power to destroy the functions that properly ought to be performed by another group within society. The manager views the firm as a servant of society to satisfy man's economic and social aspirations. The firm ought not be used to perform the functions of the political system, the legal system, or the social system.

6. The manager acts ethically as he contributes to the maintenance and creation of community by observing the processes and procedures by which goals are selected and met and conflicts are resolved. Examples of these are due process of law, the democratic process, and freedom of choice. The values and norms of justice by which people order their affairs must be respected.

7. The manager acts ethically in the organization as he demands allegiances and values that are necessary for the performance of functions within the organization. The manager who makes the organization his life and the job his reason for existence is creating another god.

*Business Power and the Community*

How should a manager use the power and resources of the business firm in society? Should he use social, economic, and political power in the interest of the maintenance of justice, peace, and the welfare of the community as a whole? We are raising questions of such nature that honesty of performance and integrity of human relations are assumed but are insufficient to provide answers. Should the business manager produce napalm for the war in Vietnam? Should the firm use its social and economic power to force people to accept racial integration?

How do we expect the manager to use the power of the organization in society? How does he conduct his activities in relationship with the systems of society? The way the organization exercises its influence can at least distort if not destroy justice between people. The manager, as he uses power, operates with two major principles:

1. The manager sees the various systems and subsystems as providing him with opportunities as well as limiting his opportunities. In the interest of justice the manager as a Christian ought not employ the power of the firm to destroy community or interfere with basic freedoms or rights.

2. The manager should accomplish the firm's goals in the social, economic, and political structures only within the framework of these systems and by the use of methods and techniques appropriate for accomplishing and changing their goals.

The manager seeking to act ethically will conduct his activities in society in the following illustrative way:

1. The manager acts ethically when he refuses to use the power of the firm to accomplish his own goals in another system. It would be unethical for him to bargain wage increases for union support in his election to a political position, or to bargain the payment of a teacher's note for a specific grade for his son. Acting ethically means using the power of the firm to accomplish the functions of the firm—for example, producing goods and services, satisfying the social demands of people within the organization, and engaging in transactions with organizations such as unions.

2. The manager acts ethically when he accepts and adheres to the goals of the other systems. The business firm is not a political organization, and the goals that are set in the political system ought to be respected and supported by the manager. The firm is acting ethically when it accepts and acts on society's desire for clean water and air, for equal-opportunity employment, for safety regulations, and for full employment.

3. The manager is acting ethically when he follows the procedures by which society's values and goals can be and are changed. Since legislation is one of the appropriate implements for change, the firm as an organization can participate in the legislative process by acting legitimately through pressure groups and professional organizations that communicate their desires to legislators or by testifying at hearings of legislative committees.

The manager is acting unethically when he endeavors to use the power of the firm to *compel* adherence to certain individual or collective values, such as requiring all employees to believe in the free-enterprise system, to wear a special-colored suit, to be clean-shaven, or to vote in a special or a certain way. The manager may ethically work for change in values and goals through participation as father, voter, citizen, or political worker or through such organizations of the social system as churches, schools, professional associations, and universities.

4. The manager is acting ethically when he observes the procedures of law and the results of the legal system, which establish norms and rules for the behavior of the firm in the social, political, legal, and ethical systems. These rules govern, for example, weights and measures, products, and mergers of firms.

5. The Christian manager is acting ethically when he refrains from using the power of the firm in society to prevent people from selecting goals, choosing alternatives, and pursuing preferences. Whether he communicates or whether he engages in transactions, the manager should not use the power of the firm to destroy other organizations in the social, political, and economic system or prevent them from meeting their goals because they do not agree with the goals of his firm. It is not the function of the firm to engage in watchdog activity over morals, social habits, and politics. It would be unethical for the manager to use the firm to destroy an organization that is acting within the law, to blackball a person because he disagrees with him, or to prevent the election of a certain party.

Justice can be secured in society only as these great concentrations of power act ethically and in the interest of justice. Justice is not secured when organizations try to accomplish that for which they are not intended. The business firm that tries to exercise political power is exercising illegitimate power, or power that has not been chosen by the people. If it uses its power to control the courts, people cannot get justice. If it uses its power to control the social system, people lose their freedoms and the ability to secure what they consider is just and right.

If we look at the business firm from the point of view of the individual in society, we expect that the firm will make it possible for people to select their goals, choose alternatives, and employ the government, the courts, and other associations and organizations that they form to meet their concepts of justice and to get what they want. The individual sees the business firm as building community when it does not use its social, economic, and political power to impose on society its own standards of justice and goodness. It has a right to expect that the business firm will operate in the interests of community and not against it. The individual can expect that the firm will not interfere with the attainment of private goals except as these are in conflict with the performance of its function.

The individual has a right to expect that the manager of a business firm will not employ the firm's power to distort the political process, to buy off judges, to use its resources to destroy the church, or to ask as a condition of employment that an individual must hold certain values.

*Business Ethics and Decision-Making*

The business manager's relationships within the firm and outside the firm involve decision-making. The manager can exercise power, accomplish goals, and employ ethics only as he makes decisions. The manager makes decisions in transactions, transformations, organizations, and communications.

No transaction can be carried on without the use of power. The question is not whether power will be used but how it should be used in transactions in the firm and in society.

The business manager or the Christian in business should exercise his power only with faith in the dignity, worth, and value of the individual. In transactions respect for the other person means that he has a right to negotiate, bargain, and exercise his free choice and his freedom. The basic conditions of honesty require that the manager or the businessman not compel people to buy a product, to force a person to work, or to deprive another person of any of his power (Fifth, Seventh, Ninth, and Tenth Commandments). The misuse of the firm's power by means of dishonesty, false information, or deceit is taking away or seeking to change the power that another person has, including his preference for a product. The Christian businessman should not distort a person's power by false and misleading information on a competitor, by withholding information, or by providing misleading alternatives. Transactions should be conducted in a spirit of freedom and honesty.

Transactions can be conducted on this level only as the conditions of the transaction are known ahead of time. Honesty requires that the conditions of exchange be made clear.

A promotion within the firm involves the exchange of money, additional prestige, and status for performance. How does one exercise honesty here? It is unethical for the Christian businessman to bargain promotions for personal values. Promotions should involve only the performance of different activities, not the requirement that a person hold new personal values. It would be unethical, for example, for a manager to bargain a promotion in exchange for the requirement that a man divorce his wife, join a lodge, associate with a different church, or join a different political party. Justice demands that the conditions of promotions be made clear and the job description accurate.

It would be unethical for businessmen who are also Christians to traffic in illegal drugs, films, and literature or to sell guns to children. Transactions must as a minimum be legal.

The business manager transforms the business firm, changes the product mix, thinks differently than he did before, hires and fires employees, and makes new and different products. The process of transformation goes on continually and is important for the variety of goods and services required. Many of the decisions are purely technical, such as purchasing a machine of *X* capacity to replace one of *Y* capacity. Should the vice-president report to the chairman of the board or to the president? Should the stockboy put the material in bins or in boxes? Should the firm produce 40 more of *X* than of *Y*? Many of these decisions are made in the interests of efficient and effective organization.

Transformations, however, involve the movement and replacement of people, including dismissal or retirement of those who are no longer useful to the firm because of old age, infirmity, or incapacity. What do the Christian convictions of the manager demand?

The Christian manager, like any manager, cannot be held responsible for the choices of people who prefer not to work, are lazy, indifferent, slothful, or careless. The real question is, What does justice demand? Does it demand that everything be weighed in the canons of efficiency?

As he deals with people in the transformation of the firm, the Christian businessman always works within the framework of respect for the dignity of the individual, using his power to direct activities, not to punish, and keeping in clear view the functions of the firm. Justice demands that efficiency be not the ultimate criterion but rather the individual. The question concerning the older employee is not whether he interferes with efficiency but whether his presence prevents the firm from performing its functions. The criterion for dismissal is what is just, fair, and honest.

The manager cannot be held responsible for changes, but he can be for the motives and methods in carrying them out. One cannot restrict change and with it the loss of jobs and opportunities if business is to meet its responsibilities to society. The ethical question is whether the business firm ought to share with the community some of the social costs of change. The answer for the ethical manager is that in the interests of justice, in the interest of community, the firm should be socially responsible for bearing its share.

The business manager works through organizations and acts within organizations. He sees organization as that which helps people accomplish goals as well as define functions and responsibilities. It is the ethical responsibility of the businessman, both as a Christian and otherwise, to accept the existence of other organizations, even if they oppose the firm, and not to destroy them. He needs to respect the arrangements and goals that people have made for organizing their affairs and activities.

The Christian businessman respects the ideology of organizational decision-making, the goals of that organization, and the structure within which decisions are made.

The Christian businessman ought not, for example, oppose the church as an organization on the grounds of its inefficiency and lack of profit. As he works in and through any organization, let him respect the differences of that organization.

The manager makes decisions in communications to which he applies standards of truthfulness, honesty, and integrity. The firm should not misrepresent its product through advertising, tell lies through public relations, nor use information as a technique and device for manipulation.

The framework of the Ten Commandments lies behind these activities. A paraphrase of a few of the Ten Commandments is illustrative:

1. I am the Lord thy God. The organization shall not become the director of people's lives but only of their activities within it. The organization shall always become a means to an end, not an end in itself. The manager shall not give to either his job or his company more than his activities, functions, and work.

2. Thou shalt not kill. The Christian manager shall respect the life, dignity, and worth of people.

3. Thou shalt not steal. The Christian manager shall not deprive a person of his power, whether social, economic, political, or legal, though that person may choose to give it up or give it away. He shall not use the power of the corporation to destroy the means or procedures by which people select their goals or seek justice and equity in society.

4. Thou shalt not covet. The Christian businessman shall not desire to take away from another person his values, faith, beliefs, rights, or duties to his home, family, country, or others by fraud, deception, or use of corporate, social, or economic power.

*The Manager and Employees*

The manager has an ethical right to direct only the functions or activities of the employee. The manager is acting unethically when he insists that the employee hold certain values that are unrelated and unnecessary for the performance of his functions in the firm.

The manager can insist that the employee hold values such as accuracy, honesty, and safety with respect to the operation of a machine for the production of bolts. He cannot insist, however, that as a condition of employment the person hold personal values in the free-enterprise system.

Respect for the dignity and worth of the individual

means that the manager acknowledges that the employee's relationship with the firm may be motivated by many goals. The manager can place limitations on only such goals as would prevent the employee from accomplishing assigned tasks. The Christian manager may feel repulsed by the employee who drinks all weekend, but he does not have a right as a condition of the employment contract to insist on sobriety on Saturday and Sunday when the person is not on the job.

The manager's responsibility to create and maintain community does not mean the development of people who all believe the same. The person who signs a contract or agrees to work for a firm has the obligation to accept direction in his behavior as an employee of that firm by the immediate superior. If he is to be fired, he can expect, and the Christian manager ought to provide for him, due process of law, a fair hearing, a right to defend himself, and honesty in his relationships.

The relationship with employees may mean that the manager will dismiss an employee. Being a Christian does not take away from the manager the right to fire, but it does take away arbitrariness, the dismissal of an employee on grounds other than unsatisfactory performance of his functions or job, and depriving the employee of his rights as a human being.

*The Christian as Businessman*

The Christian businessman directed by faith and living within the meaning of the Ten Commandments is always striving for a higher standard of justice in human relationships.

The tension he feels is not only between what is perfect and imperfect but also between his role as a businessman and his other roles and functions in society.

He is also a father, a citizen, a member of the church, an alumnus of a school or college.

The tension between his Christian commitment and his function and role in society is always meant to be constructive. He strives for the standards of morality and justice, but he is always compelled to do more, to search for more, and to strive for more. He measures his fulfillment as a businessman in society through the functions performed by the business firm as it meets its socially desirable goals, by its ability to contribute to the upbuilding of society and community, and by its satisfaction of the social and cultural goals of people.

As the Christian in business disagrees with the values and goals set by people and the way in which justice is sought, he participates in the political, social, cultural, and legal processes to remedy the wrongs and to accomplish what he believes to be right and just.

His own resources of wealth, through the stewardship of time, talents, and money, are to be placed in the service of the church and of structures in society.

The Christian in business is always in tension. He employs the resources available, but he uses them with restraint. He is a Christian and a businessman who, when he has done everything to exercise love for the advancement of justice and for the common welfare, prays, "Lord, help me; I am an unprofitable servant."

# Notes

*Chapter 1*

1. James W. Culliton, "The Problem of Ethics in Business," *Ethics in Business,* ed. Robert Bartels, Bureau of Business Research Monograph No. 111 (Columbus: Ohio State University Press, 1963), p. 5.
2. Stewart Thompson, *Management Creeds and Philosophies* (New York: American Management Association, 1958), p. 100.
3. Martin Luther, *On Trading and Usury, Works of Martin Luther,* Philadelphia Edition, IV (Philadelphia: Muhlenberg Press, 1931), p. 25.
4. Alvar O. Elbing Jr. and Carol J. Elbing, *The Value Issues of Business* (New York: McGraw-Hill Book Co., 1967), p. 217.
5. William H. Whyte Jr., *The Organization Man* (Garden City, N. Y.: Doubleday & Co., 1956), p. 7. Whyte believes that modern society has given rise to people who not only work for but *belong* to "The Organization" (p. 3). In support of their role in The Organization they have rejected the ideology of the "Protestant Ethic" with its concern for "the sacredness of property, the enervating effect of security, the virtues of thrift, of hard work and independence" (p. 5). In its place they have put a "Social Ethic," which could be called an organization ethic or a bureaucratic ethic, that "rationalizes the organization's demands for fealty" (p. 6) and makes "morally legitimate the pressures of society against the individual" (p. 7).

6. Amitai Etzioni, *Modern Organizations* (Englewood Cliffs, N. J.: Prentice-Hall, 1964), p. 3.
7. Theodore V. Houser, *Big Business and Human Values* (New York: McGraw-Hill Book Co., 1957), p. 14.

*Chapter 2*

1. *Moral and Ethical Standards in Labor and Management* (New York: National Association of Manufacturers, 1958), p. 3.
2. Henry Ford II, "Business Ethics in 1961" (private distribution), p. 11.

*Chapter 3*

1. Culliton, p. 1.
2. David H. Panitz, "Business and Ethics in the Hebrew Tradition," *Business Policy and Its Environment,* ed. Thomas Moranian, Donald Grunewald, and Richard C. Reidenbach (New York: Holt, Rinehart and Winston, 1965), p. 87.
3. Roy Oscarson, "A Commentary on Business Ethics," *Ethics and Standards in American Business,* ed. Joseph W. Towle (Boston: Houghton-Mifflin Co., 1964), p. 80.
4. John M. Hess, "Business Ethics and the Christian," *Lutheran Witness,* November 1965, p. 4.
5. Theodore Y. Yntema, *The Enrichment of Man,* Benjamin F. Fairless Memorial Lectures, 1964 (Pittsburgh: Carnegie Institute of Technology, 1965), pp. 26–27.
6. Theodore Levitt, "The Dangers of Social Responsibility," *Issues in Business and Society,* ed. William T. Greenwood (Boston: Houghton-Mifflin Co., 1964), p. 473.
7. Ibid.

8. Thomas C. Campbell Jr., "Capitalism and Christianity," in Greenwood, p. 354.
9. Thompson, p. 11.
10. Ibid., pp. 110–111.
11. Ibid., p. 110.
12. Luther, p. 22.
13. Joseph W. Towle, "Management—The Emerging Profession," in Towle, p. 264.
14. James C. Worthy, "Business and the Good Society," *The Christian in Business,* ed. Andrew J. Buehner (St. Louis: Lutheran Academy for Scholarship, 1966), p. 81.
15. "What Americans Really Think of Business," *Newsweek,* May 2, 1966, p. 85.

*Chapter 4*

1. Donald R. Heiges, *The Christian's Calling* (Philadelphia: Muhlenberg Press, 1958), p. 60.
2. Rufus Cornelsen, "Christian Faith and Economic Life," *Life in Community,* ed. Harold C. Letts (Philadelphia: Muhlenberg Press, 1957), p. 76.
3. Joseph Sittler, "The Structure of Christian Ethics," in Letts, p. 27.
4. Jaroslav Pelikan, "*Justitia* as Justice and *Justitia* as Righteousness," *Law and Theology,* ed. Andrew J. Buehner (St. Louis: Concordia Publishing House, 1965), p. 97.
5. Adolf Köberle, *Quest for Holiness* (Minneapolis: Augsburg Publishing House, 1938), p. 199.
6. Howard R. Bowen, "Ethics and Economics," in John C. Bennett et al., *Christian Values and Economic Life* (New York: Harper & Brothers, 1954), p. 191.
7. *Social Statements of the United Lutheran Church in America 1918–1962,* pp. 30–31.

# *Discussion Questions*

1. Why are the problems of business ethics more complex today than in Luther's time? What kind of ethical questions confront the modern manager that are different from those confronting an artisan who produces a product and sells it?
2. What is meant by the social responsibility of business? Do you think this is an answer to the ethical problems resulting from the power and role of business in society? Do you think businessmen should use the money and resources of the firm to support the social programs of government even if they do not agree with them?
3. What unethical practices have you observed in business? How do you think these could be eliminated? What can be done to improve business ethics?
4. What is the Christian meaning of the calling? How do you think the Christian should use the structures and forms of this world for the service of God? Do you think that being a Christian in business makes a person any less a good businessman? What duties and responsibilities are demanded of the Christian that are not asked of the non-Christian?
5. What kinds of activities does the manager perform that require ethical decisions? How does the manager act justly in the performance of these functions?
6. If the manager of a firm were acting ethically, do you think he would:
   - give money to the Community Chest?
   - fire an employee for being a Communist?
   - require that all employees vote for the same political party that he does?

- —support a lobbyist in Washington?
- —use the power and resources of the firm to prevent some social project planned by the community?
- —agree with his competitors to fix prices if the alternative were to go out of business?
- —sell people products they want even though he knows they are going to be used for illegal or immoral purposes?
- —earn as much profit as he could?

7. What would you do if, as an employee, you were instructed to foreclose a mortgage on a 75-year-old widow, which would leave her with no place to go? If you consider this ethical, how would you do your job ethically?
8. Would you ever fire an employee for any of the following reasons: old age? sickness? drunkenness? incompetence? a technological change that eliminated the job? dislike of this person?
9. What kinds of ethical standards ought to guide the manager as he performs the following activities:
   - —bargains with a union over wage increases.
   - —negotiates with customers over the price of a used car.
   - —writes a letter to his employees concerning a reorganization that will put many of them out of their jobs.
   - —decides on the marketing of a new product.
   - —decides on an advertising campaign.
10. What would you do if you were the manager of a firm and you were confronted by the following problems:

    a. A black civil rights leader has demanded that you hire 50 more Negroes within 30 days or face a total boycott of your company's products. You do not have room for 50 more employees without firing 50 white people.

b. The city council is planning to expropriate 50 acres of land that you have saved for expansion. It is suggested that this will not be expropriated if you will get rid of 10 of your employees active in the opposition party and make a large donation to the political campaign of the party in power in the community.

c. The company president has offered you a job with a big increase in salary and a promotion, but he expects you to get rid of some of your old friends, move to a different part of the community, become more active in the community by sending your children to the public school rather than church school, and join the local Masonic lodge.

d. You learn that you can get the largest sales order of your career by supporting a local group that wants to prevent the passage of an open housing law. The group is headed by a large customer of the firm, who wants you to represent the views that your firm is opposed to the open housing law. The board of directors of the company and the president are also members of the group opposed to the law.

Illustrated by Robert E. Messick